T0148633

ORPHANS *of* MUNDAKAPADAM

K.E.MATHEW, MD; FACS

WESTBOW
PRESS
A DIVISION OF THOMAS NELSON
& ZONDERVAN

Scripture taken from the Holy Bible, NEW INTERNATIONAL VERSION®.
Copyright © 1973, 1978, 1984 by Biblica, Inc. All rights reserved worldwide.
Used by permission. NEW INTERNATIONAL VERSION® and NIV® are
registered trademarks of Biblica, Inc. Use of either trademark for the offering
of goods or services requires the prior written consent of Biblica US, Inc.

WestBow Press books may be ordered through booksellers or by contacting:

WestBow Press
A Division of Thomas Nelson & Zondervan
1663 Liberty Drive
Bloomington, IN 47403
www.westbowpress.com
1 (866) 928-1240

Because of the dynamic nature of the Internet, any web addresses or
links contained in this book may have changed since publication and
may no longer be valid. The views expressed in this work are solely those
of the author and do not necessarily reflect the views of the publisher,
and the publisher hereby disclaims any responsibility for them.

Any people depicted in stock imagery provided by Thinkstock are models,
and such images are being used for illustrative purposes only.
Certain stock imagery © Thinkstock.

ISBN: 978-1-4908-5790-9 (sc)
ISBN: 978-1-4908-5791-6 (hc)
ISBN: 978-1-4908-5792-3 (e)

Library of Congress Control Number: 2014919539

Printed in the United States of America.

WestBow Press rev. date: 11/12/2014

CONTENTS

Dedicated to the precious memory of Mr. P. C. George and Sevinee Leyamma, who dedicated their life for the poor, the neglected, the sick, and the marginalized of the society in a small village, Mundakapadam, in the state of Kerala in southern India.

P. C. George   Sevinee Leyamma

Greater love has no one than this: to lay down one's life for one's friends (John 15:13).

FOREWORD

*C*hildren sometimes teach us important lessons. A little boy hardly four years old swung his leg comfortably above his head and pushed it against the chest of a boy much older than him. The act could be placed under the naughtiness of the age. However, what caught my attention was the comment he made after his disorderly act. "I was imitating the hero in a movie," he said. Watching a few scenes in the movies has somehow created a role model in his developing mind. While athletes, movie stars, and models capture the major share of the media, the giants of the scientific and socioeconomic world most of the time get the back stage.

Further unnoticed are those who deliberately forsake the rat race for success and wealth to care for the marginalized, the less privileged, and the uncared for in the world around them.

The author, Dr. K. E. Mathew, has done a magnificent job in bringing to the attention of the new generation the life and work of Mr. P. C. George and Miss Leyamma Cheriyan, who comforted and blessed many lives ignored by the society. The task is difficult indeed when such great lives shunned publicity and left few published documents about them. From the pages of the journal of Mr. P. C. George, his letters to his nephews and nieces, and a few Malayalam books, the author has brought to the attention of the readers the saintly lives of P. C. George Sir and Leyamma Kochamma.

While shooting stars make an interesting sight in the skies, the permanent shining stars in the sky light up the firmament.

Mr. P. C. George and his sister are forever lovely stars in the firmament of eternity. The continuance of the Mundakapadam Mandiram as a model institution and its ministry of care is God's endorsement of these saintly lives.

It has been my privilege to know the author, Dr. K. E. Mathew, for many years from my childhood. As a disciplined young man and a model student, he went through tough training of the medical school to become an excellent surgeon. For many years, he used the surgeon's scalpel to physically heal many, and now his pen portrays heroes of yesteryear to challenge the new generation to live for a higher goal in life. The author shares a compassionate heart for the needy, similar to the lives he portrays through this book.

It is my prayer that many in this generation will find a role model to follow to make this world a better place to live.

"Those who are wise will shine like the brightness of the heavens, and those who lead many to righteousness, like the stars for ever and ever" (Daniel 12:3–4).

Dr. George Cherian
General Secretary
Missions India
missionsindia.org

PREFACE

The meaning and purpose of suffering, especially the suffering of the innocent, has been an enigma.

When writing to the church in Corinth, the apostle Paul stated: "Blessed be the God and father of our Lord Jesus Christ, the father of mercies and God of all comfort, who comforts us in all our tribulations, that we may be able to comfort those who are in any trouble, with the comfort with which we ourselves are comforted by God" (2 Corinthians 1:3–4).

The story of the orphans of Mundakapadam is a story of God revealing His purpose through the lives of a bunch of kids who became orphans at an early age in a remote village in southern India during the first half of the twentieth century. It is the story of one beggar going out to bring other beggars to the source of bread that he found. It is the story of faith, prayer, love for God, and love for neighbor as well as total submission to the will of God and the leading of the Holy Spirit.

George, Chackochy, Kochu Kochu, and Pennamma are the four heroes of faith in the story. Their love for each other and for God led them to love their fellow men and women that were poor, sick, or rejected by family and friends. Pennamma (Leyamma), the youngest, dedicated her whole life for serving the destitute. Her three brothers, teachers by profession, were shining examples of the "priesthood of all believers."

The tears, tribulations, poverty, and hunger that George and Leyamma went through as orphans prepared them for a great mission—to serve the poor and destitute. God gave them big dreams and considerable supporters and friends who also were dreamers for God. The result was Mandiram (which means *home*), providing living quarters for over 150 destitute people. The location also includes a library; a chapel; assisted-living facilities for the elderly and the lonely; retirement homes; a Baalika bhavan for serving little girls; a multi-specialty, full-service hospital providing free medical care to the residents of Mandiram; a school of nursing; a psychiatric hospital; and a palliative care unit that provides supportive and spiritual care for the terminally ill.

Many in the local community were partners in the service project from its planning stage onward. Bible study and prayer groups that were led by P. C. George created a large number of disciples for the Lord. Social programs went a long way in saving many a family from the ill effects of alcoholism. Numerous youngsters got proper guidance in life and became productive citizens. Now there is a large number of supporters for Mandiram all across the globe helping with prayer and financial support.

I had deliberated on the idea of publishing a book on Mr. P. C. George and his sister Leyamma. P. C. George was a visionary and a man ahead of his time. He and his younger sister, with limited resources, achieved more in their short life span than many did with unlimited resources and longer life spans. Someone commented that if these two siblings had belonged to the Catholic Church, they would have had a chance to be declared saints. Through their lives in a little-known village at a time when there were very few avenues for publicity, they demonstrated their love for fellow human beings through actions and words. Everyone has a story to tell, and each story is different from the other. Very few books have been published on the lives of these two people, and most of them are in Malayalam. Annual reports and souvenirs from Mandiram have done a good job in publishing articles from time to time on the life of the founders, George and Leyamma.

My association with Mandiram was through my wife, Leyamma, who happened to be the niece of George and of Leyamma, her namesake! After our marriage in December 1971, we stayed in the renovated home of George and Leyamma, close to Mandiram, for almost one year. I had the privilege to get to know all the sevinees (female caregivers) in Mandiram who started their career with Leyamma and P. C. George. The zeal and dedication that Leyamma had instilled in them continued to be strong. Men and women who had worked with or had personal contact with George and Leyamma were still around, talking about these great lives. There were several cousins and friends of the founders living within walking distance from the Mandiram campus. Kollanthara Chackochy, Kalayil Pappy, and the Nagapuram siblings—N. K. Chacko (Kocu), N. K. Mariamma (Pennamma), N. K. Thomas (Thommachan), N. K. John (Johnny)—are a few. I spent evenings with many of them, listening to their firsthand stories about Mandiram and its founders. The more I learned about P. C. George and Leyamma the more resolved I became about making their story known to the younger generation. Our children are the second generation to follow them. Sadly, they know very little about their great ancestors.

I was fortunate enough to get access to the very few personal letters from P. C. George addressed to his nephew and namesake George Cheriyan, my wife's eldest brother, known as Georgekuttychayan. These handwritten letters are well preserved and treasured by Georgekuttychayan. A couple of these letters are published in this book. They will give the readers a chance to see and feel P. C. George talking to the younger generation. In spite of a busy life and many health issues, George was taking time to write to his nieces and nephew. Through these letters, he showed his love and concern for them, and he instructed them on valuable lessons in life. He also commended them on their achievements in school or at home. In spite of the many technological advances in communication in the modern day, these handwritten letters take the top spot on my list over any number of e-mails and phone calls, or even FaceTime calls!

Georgekuttychayan was a treasure of information and anecdotes about the life of his uncle and aunt. Thanks also to Georgekuttychayan for the tremendous support and the part he continues to play as a role model to the rest of the family.

My sincere thanks also go to the Rev. Dr. K. C. Mathew of Mandiram for the support and encouragement he gave me when I told him about my intention to write a book on the founders of Mandiram. The annual reports of Mandiram and other articles he gave me were very helpful.

It was not by chance that Dr. George Cherian wrote the foreword for the book. Dr. Cherian's dad, the late Mr. K. V. Cherian, was a friend of P. C. George and also was active in ecumenical fellowship. George Cherian, a well-qualified engineer who was holding a financially secure secular job, heard God's call twenty-five years ago and followed Him. George Cherian is busy serving the poor and marginalized in many parts of India through orphanages, old-age homes, medical clinics, and schools while teaching the Word of God. He emulates P. C. George in many ways. I thank George Cherian for the continued prayerful support and encouragement.

I thank the many friends of P. C. George and Leyamma who helped me with historical information about them and many who displayed to me the spirit of mission in their own lives.

It was my wife, Leya, who introduced me to this family with the noble heritage. She has been my pillar of support. She wrote a chapter that appears in this book. I can never thank her enough for all the love and support she gives me.

The few books that are published about P. C. George or Leyamma are all in Malayalam and not read by the younger generation. My earnest prayer is that this book will fill that void.

Multifaceted activities initiated by George and Leyamma saw a steady growth, thanks to the support and prayers of friends and well-wishers. Mundakapadam Mandirangal proudly declare the story of

P. C. George and Leyamma. The buildings for the hospital, school of nursing, psychiatric wing, Mandiram chapel, office, residential quarters for sevinees, better living quarters for the residents of Mandiram, and many assisted-living quarters fill the campus. And the spirit of selfless service continues to pour out from those who still work in these facilities. Support from the friends of Mandiram all across the globe helps to supplement the many sacrificial gifts from inside the country. Now we can watch the activities at Mandiram via Google from anywhere in the world by searching for mandiram.org.

CHAPTER 1

Orphans of Mundakapadam

"Appa, can you tell another story?" It was our youngest granddaughter calling out from the back seat of the minivan. We were returning home after dinner at a friend's home. Our daughter and son-in-law were away at a meeting. It was one of the rare chances when my wife and I, as grandparents, could spend time with our grandchildren. I had exhausted my stock of stories on the way to the dinner. So I had to make up another story or come up with something new.

After thinking for a minute, I asked, "Caroline, do you know who an orphan is?"

"Is it not someone who lost both mother and father," she asked.

"Very good; you are right," I said. "I am going to tell you the story of a bunch of orphans from India. Pay attention, because it is going to be the story of some people who are very close to you."

With this brief introduction, I commenced narrating the story of the orphans of Mundakapadam. Once upon a time, there was a young couple living in a small village, Mundakapadam, in the state of Kerala in southern India. They were from the lower middle class, enjoying the peaceful and quiet life of that agricultural village. Though not wealthy by worldly standards, they had a rich heritage of Christian values and high moral and ethical standards. As this couple did not have a child, they started to pray for a son. They even pleaded with God, promising to dedicate their son for God's work.

And a boy was born to this couple. They named him George. Soon two more boys were born, and then a girl. The second boy was Chackochy, and the youngest boy was named Kochu Kochu. The girl was Pennamma and was also called Leyamma.

When George, the oldest, was twelve years old and Leyamma, the youngest, was only four, the children's parents both died within a few months of each other. The care of these four children fell squarely on the shoulders of their mom's parents, who were already up in age and not in the best of health. They took charge of the boys and the young girl. These grandparents helped the children in their studies and taught them Bible stories. They showed them how to love their neighbors and those who were less fortunate than themselves.

Unfortunately, by the time George was sixteen and Leyamma was eight, their grandfather died after a brief illness. Grandmother was already a sick person. When people returned home after the funeral of the grandfather, they found Grandmom dead too.

George had to step up to the plate and assume the responsibility of taking care of his younger siblings. By this time he had graduated from high school; he had obtained training to be a teacher. He became a teacher in a school a couple of miles away from home. With the small salary, George managed to send his siblings to school and to provide for the food and other needs of the family. Also, he found time and resources to take care of the poor and destitute in the village. He got involved in the public health and cultural matters of the community. George took an active interest in helping people to escape alcohol addiction and showed the poor people how to be wise in finances.

Leyamma decided to work along with George in his social and altruistic activities. In fact, she remained unmarried and dedicated her whole life for the care of the destitute. She encouraged George to bring home the people near death from the street to their home. There she would try to nurse them to health. With the hard work of Leyamma and George and the help of good friends around the area, they were able to open a home for the destitute in a small way. Leyamma, along with a few dedicated volunteer workers, called sevinees, took care of their every need. These few performed cooking, cleaning, and bathing, while also dressing wounds. They obtained medications and administered them. They took care of those who were on their deathbeds and then cleaned the bodies and arranged funerals.

During one rainy season, there was an outbreak of cholera in the village. An elderly man who was brought to the home with severe diarrhea died. Leyamma took care of him and helped in the funeral. The next day she too became sick. In spite of all the care and help from friends and medical personnel, Leyamma died of cholera. She was only thirty-one years old!

Poor George was in deep sorrow. His resolve to continue serving the poor only got firmer. Soon he had another agenda. He wanted to open a hospital. He believed that if there had been adequate medical help, his dear sister would not have met with the untimely death. This resolve resulted in planning for and finally opening a simple hospital. This was a smaller version of what today is a larger and more modern facility called Mandiram Hospital! P. C. George was a visionary, way ahead of his time. He did a lot more than one person normally can do in a lifetime. He, too, died early, at the age of fifty-one.

And do you know what happened to the other two boys in the family? Both of them got a good education in spite of financial burdens and the absence of parental support. Both of them became teachers. Kochu Kochu became a pastor in Mar Thoma Church and served the church while developing a residential school and working there as the principal for several decades. Leyamma found a bride for her brother, the Rev. P. C. Cheriyan, and the couple had nine children. The oldest was a boy, whom they named George after P. C. George. And they named their fourth baby Leyamma.

"Appa, Amma's name is Leyamma too!" exclaimed Madison, our second grandchild.

"Amma's brother is George too," Joshua, the oldest grandson added.

"Yes," I said, "and their father, your grandfather, is Rev. P. C. Cheriyan. And his siblings are P. C. Chacko, P. C. George, and Leyamma."

"Oh, now we know why you told us that this is our story," Joshua said.

"Appa, this is the best story you ever told us!" Madison exclaimed.

"Stay tuned," I said. "There is more to come on the orphans of Mundakapadam."

CHAPTER 2

Mundakapadam of Yesteryear

*I*t is very important to learn about the socioeconomic conditions in the Mundakapadam of yesteryear before we learn more about George and Leyamma. This village in the suburbs of Kottayam, in central Travancore, got its name from two words, *Mundakan* and *padam*, the former a variety of rice and the latter meaning "the field." Essentially it was a collection of rice fields in this village that gave it the name. This agricultural village had all sorts of crops: rice, tapioca, and coconut, along with black pepper and other spices.

Most of the villagers were poor or near the poverty line. The majority were able to make ends meet, but any medical or financial emergency situation often threw them off balance and into unbearable burdens. These could include high interest debts or selling themselves into servanthood forever.

The caste system was very much alive. People from lower castes were not welcome in the homes of those in the higher castes. Ezhavas could come up to the courtyard while Pulayas and Parayas had no access to the courtyard. The untouchables, when walking on public streets, had to call out "*hoy, hoy,*" warning the upper class of their presence so as to avoid desecration. On encountering anyone from the upper caste, these unfortunate men and women had to jump off from the street and into the bushes or the dirty ditches and hide until the "holy one" passed.

Most of the villagers followed one form or another of a religion. The majority were Hindus; the caste system originated in Hinduism and was perpetuated by its hierarchy.

Alcoholism and a variety of types of drug abuse were prevalent. This resulted in the sending of many families into utter poverty; and for a lot more, it caused the breakdown of their family unit.

Christianity in Kerala traces its origin back to the first century, when one of the twelve disciples of Jesus, Saint Thomas, landed in this southern state in India and converted some families to the Christian faith. The arrival of Vasco da Gama to the shores of northern Kerala in 1498 opened the door for further spread of Christianity to this region. For the next couple of centuries, Catholicism saw a steady growth. This was a difficult time for the Syrian Christians in Kerala. Many of their customs and practices in worship were unpalatable to the Catholic hierarchy, who wanted to completely westernize the local church. This led to many protests including the "Koonan kurisu treaty," where a huge crowd of protesters held onto a long rope that was tied to a large cross, making it tilt, while they proclaimed their independence from the pope. By the late eighteenth and early nineteenth centuries, Protestant missionaries of various denominations (such as Lutheran; Baptist) and organizations (such as Basel Mission; Church Mission Society) showed their presence in Kerala. It was their hard work that led to establishment of English schools, translation of Bible into local languages, and the elevation of awareness about social evils among the people in Kerala.

The town of Kottayam, near Mundakapadam, reaped the benefit of the work of these missionaries who helped to open the Church Mission Society (CMS) high school and seminary for theological education. The names of missionaries such as David Wordsworth, Walker, Grigson, and Nagal are worth mentioning here. Prayer meetings and group Bible studies that attracted many were conducted in and around the town.

Mundakapadam, too, witnessed a revival during this time. Several Christian families in the village came together for regular Bible study and worship. Their friendship extended further into cooperative farming, a brand new idea for the village. Though not rich in material sense, they all were rich in virtues and Christian values.

George and Leyamma's family, the Puthuparambil family, was right at the center of this small group. Their mother, Kuttiyamma, and their father, Cheriyan, with the four children, formed a model family. They were well liked by everyone in the village.

Cheriyan owned a pair of oxen and a bullock cart that carried loads to the high ranges. Roads were rough and unsafe with robbers, and persons hauling loads always traveled as a caravan. Though the caravan members were of differing religious backgrounds, they always wanted Cheriyan to pray at the beginning as well as at the end of their journey.

In the Puthuparambil home, there was family prayer in the morning and evening. They attended Bible study and prayer meetings during the weekdays and church services on Sundays. Friends and neighbors made it a point to go for these as a group. Their friendship was evident, even at their farms where they plowed the field, planted, and harvested as a group. Cooperative planting of this type was otherwise unheard of at that time in that area. Cheriyan used his cart to transport the agricultural products to the market.

In his diary notes, P. C. George in later years related an incident in his childhood that had made him proud of his father. One evening, when George was five years old, he rode with his dad on the cart when Cheriyan was delivering a load of rice in several sacks to someone in the nearby village. When the steward of the house announced their arrival to the master of the house, the master ordered the steward to measure the rice and take it in. Before they started measuring, the master realized that it was Cheriyan who had brought the load and decided against checking the accuracy of the measurement. He told his steward, "If Cheriyan brings the load, you don't have to measure it." To the young boy, what a tremendous testimony this was for his dad!

Kuttiyamma, the children's mom, was a God-fearing person too. As a young girl she had enjoyed the Bible studies and prayer meetings. After one such meeting, Kuttiyamma came home and made the following note in the margin of her Bible: "Kuttiyamma Died." Her father did not understand what this meant, and he did not like the idea of scribbling notes in the Holy Book either. Only Kuttiyamma knew that through her note that day she was joining the apostle Paul in Galatians 2:20, where he boldly stated: "I have died, but Christ lives in me. And now I live by faith in the Son of God, who loved me and gave his life for me."

Not long after their marriage, the Cheriyan–Kuttiyamma couple was blessed with the birth of a baby who soon died. This threw them into deep sorrow. Furthermore, Kuttiyamma found she could not get pregnant, and this continued a few years. They were praying intensely for a baby, and Kuttiyamma made a promise to God that if they were blessed with children, they would dedicate them to His service. That is exactly what this couple later did. Soon they were blessed with the birth of their eldest son, George, on April 15, 1901. Two more boys followed—Chackochy and Kochu Kochu—and then a girl, Pennamma. All of them were in His ministry in various forms.

God immensely blessed the family and their posterity. They became a blessing to many, and the story continues. It is the story of the orphans of Mundakapadam, the story of God in His wisdom taking and using the Puthuparambil orphans to be a blessing to many more orphans. The much afflicted would become the consolation for the much afflicted. With the apostle Paul, they could say, "Blessed be the God of all consolation who consoles us in all our afflictions, so that we may be able to console those who are in any affliction with the consolation with which we ourselves were consoled by God" 2 Corinthians 1:2–4 (NRSV).

George and his siblings began their life in Mundakapadam, a place that was truly in need of a transformation from within. Almighty God had special plans for their life, and He was going to show them His plans in due time!

George was enrolled in the Machucadu CMS primary school, where he studied for four years. He was intelligent and hardworking. The school was about one kilometer from his home, and he walked to and from school along with a few of his friends. From early childhood onward, he loved to take care of anyone in need.

One afternoon on his way home, he saw an elderly woman in rags lying on the sidewalk. She probably had been thrown out of her home in her old age, and with no one to look after her, she had walked around begging till she fell on the roadside and was left to die there. Like the man in Jesus' story of the Good Samaritan, George had compassion on this woman. He and his friends decided to do what they could. They erected a temporary shed over the woman with a few poles and coconut leaves, to protect her from the elements. They brought porridge from home and fed her. She lasted only a couple of days more, but when she died, there were loving and caring boys around her—probably for the first time in a long time. George and his friends made arrangements for her funeral also by getting the help of a local evangelist.

Looking back, one can wonder: Was this woman the first recipient of hospice care in Mundakapadam? Was she the first client of the home for the poor that was yet to come? Was that temporary shed at the side of Puthuppally–Kottayam Road, not too far from the present Mandiram Junction, the foreshadowing of the Mandiram that was yet to be built?

Just as George was proud of his parents, they were proud of their son. One evening, Kuttiyamma sent George to Puthuppally to buy something from the shop. On his way home, he met an elderly lady carrying a load of firewood on her head, walking very slowly under the weight. He had pity on her and offered to carry the load for her. The woman obliged. With the heavy load over his head,

George walked with her toward her destination. He persevered in carrying that load for the poor woman for almost a mile, and then he ran home to his mom. She was waiting anxiously for the son who had gone for a short assignment and been late! On hearing the story, Kuttiyamma was proud of her son. She hugged him and thanked God.

Furthermore, George, in his journals, made this comment: "If I have another life on this earth, I want to be at Mundakapadam with the same parents." He and his siblings received all the Christian virtues and love along with proper training from Cheriyan and Kuttiyamma.

Unfortunately, Kuttiyamma passed away at the young age of thirty-two, when George was only twelve and Leyamma four. Cheriyan, too, did not live very long.

The care of the four children fell squarely on the shoulders of their maternal grandparents, Kochu Varghese and Achiyamma. These grandparents had established a strong bond with their grandchildren early in their lives. By reading to them and telling stories to them, Kochu Varghese established a lasting bond with the grandkids. He too was well-respected in the village and was always available for any one in need.

However, the death of the children's mother, their daughter, followed by the untimely passing of their son-in-law, threw the older couple into deep sorrow and depression. Achiyamma was already sickly and bedridden. Kochu Varghese, too, became ill and bedridden with dysentery and died. While his body was being taken away to the cemetery, Achiyamma called out from her bed: "Are you going away, leaving me here like this?"

When the funeral for Kochu Varghese was over and the relatives returned home, Achiyamma had already followed her husband in death! They wanted to be together, even in death!

George and his siblings were left with a few neighbors as supporters and sympathizers. God, who takes care of the orphans, was with them, as we will see soon.

God sent several of His angels in human form to serve His children at the right time. While George was taking care of his grandfather on his sickbed, a prominent fellow in the community had come to visit him. He was Range Inspector of Schools Rao Sahib O. M. Cherian. He had learned from George's grandfather that George had appeared for the seventh grade examination. After the grandparents had passed away and the examination result was out, Mr. O. M. Cherian sent a letter to George through another person. This was the appointment order asking George to assume duty as a teacher at the Puthuppally school the following day! With a thankful heart, George joined his job. As he did not have a shirt, he had to go with a dhoti around his waist and a shawl on his shoulder. Because George was so young looking, initially the headmaster mistook him for a student coming for admission to the school and told him that there was no room for him there!

CHAPTER 3

Life at Home and the Beginning of Mandiram

A typical kitchen in those days was entirely different from what we have now, especially the ones we are used to in the Western world. There was no electricity. Just imagine living without the electric gadgets from our present-day kitchen! That will give you some idea what life was like then.

There was another big difference compared to modern times: a man's place was always outside the kitchen! From dawn to dusk and into the night, the woman of the house was in her kitchen. The fire in the kitchen never went out. All through the day there would be one or more pots on the hearth. After dinner, when the cooking for the day was done, the fire was maintained simmering in a pot.

Before the next day dawned, Mom would resume cooking. When it was necessary to restart the fire, it was a major task. The rest of the family would wake up to the aroma of freshly made coffee. Most people owned a cow, a buffalo, or a goat that provided the milk. The lady of the house usually milked the animal.

Then it would be time for breakfast. And lunches would be prepared and packed for the kids going to school. After that came the planning and preparing of lunch, then tea and a snack, and then dinner!

Often a visitor would pop in without notice. Remember, they did not have texting or faxing or the use of a telephone then. If a black crow kept on crowing in a peculiar way, they knew that was an advance warning of the arrival of a guest. If a cat sat up and cleaned its face with its paws, that would indicate a guest was on his or her way. There would always be leftover rice in the bottom of the pot for a guest who walked in or for a beggar who asked for food.

After dinner, the mother would pour water over the leftover rice and keep it overnight in the *uri* (a two- or three-tier storage device utilizing three ropes that is hung from a beam in the kitchen). Food that was hung in the *uri* was not easily accessible to the cat, mouse, or chicken that frequently passed through the kitchen in search of food.

The grinding, chopping, and crushing of the grains and vegetables were done by hand!

Getting rice harvested and ready for cooking was a long process, and it too was the responsibility of the housewife. The raw grain would be dried under the sun first, then boiled and dried again. Then it was milled in a special stone mill (*ural*) and pounded with four-foot-long cylindrical wooden sticks with metal rims at the end (*ulakka*). The husk and rice would be separated by rhythmically moving the grain inside a flat pan (*muram*). The cleaned-up rice would be ready for cooking.

Rice can be ground into powder to make pancakes and other snacks, and the elaborate job of making them would fall on the shoulders of the housewife!

Coconuts that were harvested would be stored near the kitchen. The coconut would be shelled, and a *chirava* would be used to shred the coconut for cooking. The coconut shells were kept aside for making wooden spoons or for use as fuel for the fire in the hearth.

Cooking was a full-time job. With no refrigeration or cold storage, nearly every meal had to be freshly made. What a chore!

The kitchen had only limited pieces of furniture. The family sat on very low stools called *koranti*. They ate the food from enameled metal plates and used large saucers for drinks.

Kerosene lamps were made of brass. They had to be cleaned and polished; also, the oil was refilled and the wicks trimmed. At dusk these lamps were lit and placed in strategic places inside the home to brighten it.

None of the houses in the village had cemented floors or a tiled roof. The floors and often the walls were made out of mud, beaten and leveled using a handheld wooden piece called *nilam thally*. Every couple of weeks, the floor had to be hand polished with a mixture of cow dung and charcoal. Once this had dried up, the floor provided a cool, comfortable surface upon which to sit or lie down.

George took charge of the household and his siblings. His meager salary was barely enough to provide for their daily lives, let alone the fees for their education. George insisted that his siblings get the best education possible, and he made the sacrifices to make that happen by teaching students in the early morning and after school in order to earn extra income.

George also organized the youth in the village and taught them life skills and primary health habits.

Leyamma was enrolled in the government primary school at Machucadu until she was in her fifth grade. She missed classes and often was late for exams because of her responsibilities at home. After a couple of unsuccessful attempts at the fifth grade examination, Leyamma decided to quit school and remain at home, working full time. Her prayer life, Bible reading, and study of God's Word continued.

When her older brother came home in the evening and described his encounters with the poor and destitute on the roadside, Leyamma's heart would fill with compassion. She would ask George why he did not bring them home so that they could feed and care for them. She was quite supportive of George's altruistic activities.

Leyamma did the nursing care, cooking, and feeding of the needy. George helped to do the washing in a nearby stream. The local dhobies refused to wash the clothes of the destitute, as many of them had dreaded infections. A few ladies from the neighborhood who knew Leyamma, and some her relatives, came and helped them. Initially some worked during the day and later others volunteered to join as full-time workers. Ultimately, many of them would work at Mandiram for years until their death. A few remain today, spending their old age, many of them in poor health, at Mandiram.

My wife, Leyamma, had the privilege to live with these Sevini Kochammas for a few months while working at Mandiram Hospital as a junior doctor. After our marriage we moved into the original Puthuparambil house next to Mandiram. During our yearlong stay there, I got the opportunity to enjoy the hospitality of these devoted servants of God, and I listened to their stories of struggles in the formative years of this ministry.

It was heartwarming to hear them sharing their devotion to Kunchayan (George) and Leyamma during their difficult years at Mandiram. These sevinees were full-time volunteers, and they cared for every need of the residents. They were the cooks, the cleaners, the nurses, the pharmacists, the spiritual leaders, and the disciplinarians as well as the undertakers.

They collected agricultural produce from nearby villages during the harvest season. Taking care of older men and women from different backgrounds was not an easy task. Quarrels and clashes between the residents were not uncommon. There was petty stealing. And false accusations were made against the sevinees. It is a wonder how these special women withstood the difficulties and faithfully carried out their duties to their Master for several decades without any monetary benefit. It is through people like these that the work that was started by George and Leyamma can be continued. These angels with no wings were never in the forefront or in the limelight. They are waiting for the Master's commendation: "Well done my faithful servants!"

A few inmates of Mandiram, 1976

Chapter 4

Leyamma: A Dedicated Life

$\mathcal{A}$fter Leyamma stopped attending school, she was sent to the Vanitha Mandiram (which means Women's Home) in Thiruvalla, where she received training under the Australian pioneer missionary Gwendoline Jane Kellaway. Vanitha Mandiram was a Bible school, established in 1925, and Gwendoline, often called Gwen, was its founding principal. It trained women in Bible studies and in homemaking. Gwendoline, who was born to the Rev. Alfred Charles Kellaway in Melbourne, Australia, had decided to migrate to southern India at the age of twenty-five to serve and educate women.

Gwen Kellaway had a profound influence on Leyamma. During the training in Vanitha Mandiram, Leyamma traveled to the northern part of Kerala to work in the mission center in Palghat. She was trained in various aspects of missions and witnessing. And it was in Vanitha Mandiram that she met Kunjamma from Thalavady, another young lady who would later be recommended as the bride for her brother Kochu Kochu, the Rev. P. C. Cheriyan.

Leyamma returned to Mundakapadam with a full dedication to serve the poor and to assist her brother George in his endeavors.

One evening after dinner, when Leyamma had been home from Vanitha Mandiram for a couple of days, she and George had a conversation. It can be summarized as follows:

GEORGE: "Pennamma, I think that we should open an Agathi Mandiram."

LEYAMMA: "What is an Agathi Mandiram, Kunjichayan?"

GEORGE: "It is a home for those who have no home and no one to take care of them."

LEYAMMA: "But who is going to take care of them?"

GEORGE: "You will be cooking for them and feeding them; you will be cleaning their wounds and nursing them; and you will be washing their clothes and caring for them."

LEYAMMA: "Kunjichayan, I don't know how to do all that. Still, I want to help."

GEORGE: "I will give my salary for buying food for them. On weekends we will go from house to house begging for help for these people and get the necessary help."

LEYAMMA: "I will do as much as I can. Let us go to bed now. They say that the plans one makes after dinner usually won't materialize!"

Ultimately this plan did materialize.

As Leyamma was completing her training in Vanitha Mandiram, there was serious discussion about starting Agathi Mandiram in Manganam. Several of the supporters met with George. When there was a question as to who would manage the difficult day-to-day affairs of Mandiram, several of the youth volunteers came forward. As to who would be the woman to take care of the residents, George volunteered the service of his sister Leyamma.

One evening there was an unexpected guest at the Puthuparambil home. An elderly gentleman, very sick with diarrhea and barely able to walk, approached the home, begging for help. He had no place to go and no one to care for him. George and Leyamma took Ayyappan into their thatched prayer shed next to their home. George bought a cot for twenty-two *chakkram*, the coin for monetary transactions in Travancore, and brought it home. They nursed Ayyappan on that cot, feeding and caring for him. In a few days, he was well. He decided to stay with them, and for many years to come, he did little odd jobs here and there to help them.

After Ayyappan, there came to Mandiram another gentleman, Varkey, who was an amputee. He had been rejected by all and had engaged in begging for several years.

As the number of the needy increased, there was a great need to move their abode to another freestanding building. A thatched shed was constructed, and residents were accommodated in it.

Leyamma had to do all the nursing care, cooking, and feeding. George was there to help in washing their clothes in a nearby stream. The local dhobies refused to wash the clothes of the residents of Mandiram, as many of them had dreaded infections. Soon Leyamma received assistance from some of her relatives as well as a few ladies from the neighborhood who knew Leyamma well. Initially some of these women helped by working in Mandiram during the daytime, while living at their own homes. Later on, a few volunteered to join as full-time workers in Mandiram. The names of some of them are mentioned in other anecdotes in this book. The volunteers, known as sevinees, worked in Mandiram for many years, and most of them died there. A few are still at Mandiram, spending their old age in poor health.

It is worth mentioning in some detail the type of residents or "inmates" that Mandiram received in the initial period and the trouble that was encountered in taking care of their needs. Leyamma and her helpers were prepared for anything that was thrown their way.

A sixty-two-year-old gentleman with ulcers all over his body, making him scratch intensely, was going around begging. He was in deep depression and tried to end his life by jumping in the river. The poor fellow was rescued from the water and was brought to Mandiram.

A woman in old age was too senile even to remember her own name and was incontinent; she had to be nursed on the bed like a little baby.

Boys who were fighting with dogs for the food thrown in the ditches around the restaurants in Kottayam were rescued and brought to Mandiram.

There was a gentleman who had worked hard every day in the rubber plantations in the high ranges for twenty years; he came to the town of Kottayam with a blanket and malaria as his only savings. He too became an inmate in Mandiram. There was an infant rescued when she was found breastfeeding on her poor mother who was lying unconscious in the ditch by the side of the road. Also brought in was a woman, nearly one hundred years old, who had lost all of her eight children, was destitute, and was bent down like a bow, using a walking cane. There were several men and women with advanced cancer with foul-smelling ulcers over the face and elsewhere who were chased away from their homes and neighborhood but who finally found refuge in Mandiram. There were paralytics, blind, those who were rejected by relatives, those who had lost all children in death—everyone had a sad story and a very sad background.

Mandiram, originally intended for five residents, already had fifty. Washing and cleaning the residents' clothes, mats, and cots, feeding them, and giving their medications on time were not easy chores. Several needed to be spoon fed; some needed hot water for a bath; some needed assistance to sit up and even to change their position in bed. Cleaning and sanitizing the rooms, consoling each person in their troubles, wiping their tears, massaging and closing the eyes in death, bathing the dead and arranging the burial—all of these tasks fell squarely on the shoulders of the few sevinees.

In a letter to a friend, Leyamma talked about the continual work: "The constant back ache that I am experiencing now is the direct result of all the hard work in the past and not the present work. Even though we had some helpers in the past, I had to be always in the forefront. Now everyone knows her part of the job. My coworkers are showing more love and sympathy to me these days. As they know that I had worked hard in the past, now they won't let me do anything if I am not feeling well."

No One Wants To Die Alone

Attending to those in their deathbed was the most difficult job. A lady from North Paravoor with her four-year-old daughter was admitted to Mandiram in very bad shape. The woman's whole body bloated up with fluid, and she was not able to eat. Breathing, too, became hard. She was very much aware of her impending death, and the prospect of leaving her daughter caused her intense pain. She repeatedly verbalized her concern as to who would take care of her daughter once she was gone. On March 1, the girl was sleeping on the floor in a corner of her mom's room. Around midnight, the woman gestured to get her daughter onto her bed. She repeatedly caressed and kissed the girl and shed tears on her. Leyamma was watching all this. She told the lady, "Janaki, entrust your daughter to the almighty Lord."

Janaki responded by praying, "Lord, I entrust my baby to your hands." There was peace on Janaki's face after this. She let Leyamma carry the sleeping girl and put her on the floor. In a short while, the girl woke up, crying, as if someone had shaken her to wake her up. Janaki had gone by then to her eternal abode.

Leyamma's thoughts wandered into her own past. Over twenty years earlier, as a four-year-old girl, she too woke up one dark night and cried for the whole day and more. Her dear mother had left Leyamma and gone to her eternal home at the young age of thirty-one. She too had entrusted Leyamma and her siblings to the Lord's service, even before any of them were born. She too had prayed for her and her siblings. The prayer of mothers never goes unanswered. And the tears they shed in prayers for their children will be transformed into showers of blessings on them. In Leyamma's case, her own mother's prayers had been at work in making Leyamma a source of comfort to many. Otherwise, how would someone get the courage to be with a dying mother and tell her the right words at the right time: "Janaki, entrust your daughter into the hands of Almighty God."

Little did Leyamma realize that God had already planned great things for Janaki's little girl: That she would have caregivers in Mandiram, and that Leyamma's own brother Kochayan (the Rev. P. C. Cheriyan) and family and his children—all nine of them—would treat the girl as if she were the oldest sibling and address her as Marykutty. And that she would be serving generations of destitutes passing through the portals of Mandiram for several decades to come. This is the story of Marykutty—just one among many whom God touched through the service of Leyamma, one orphan of Mundakapadam touching another orphan in God's name!

No one wants to die alone. Having someone close by to provide consolation and comfort is a great blessing. In Leyamma, Janaki got the support she needed. Even our Lord Jesus had a few of His close friends and relatives close by when He was dying on the cross. He, too, got the chance to entrust His dear mother into the hands of His close friend and confidant John. I often wonder about all those men and women who spent their final days and dying moments on earth on ventilators and life support systems in seclusion in the intensive care units, away from their dear ones. If they had a choice, I think they would have preferred to be surrounded by their dear ones in the familiar surroundings of their homes.

The sacrificial service of Leyamma and friends in Mandiram was rewarded by the more-than-expected cooperation from people all around. Several dignitaries from all over India visited Mandiram and recorded their satisfactory comments. Mr. K. P. S. Menon, Sir C. P. Ramaswamy Iyer, Dr. T. H. Somerwell, as well as Dr. E. F. Paton of Thirupathoor Asramam were among the prominent visitors during this period. Several Sunday schools from around the state brought their students to visit Mandiram and interact with the residents.

During harvest time, many people contributed a portion of their harvest for Mandiram. Many decided to contribute money and to support Mandiram activities on a regular basis. Volunteers were busy going out to collect the contributions from the supporters all around

Mundakapadam. There are not many public institutions that gained such widespread support in such a short time as Mandiram did.

Mandiram's rapid growth and progress brought in more problems too. There were visitors to Mandiram day in and day out. Supporters and prospective residents and prospective volunteers came from far and wide. It was mainly the responsibility of Leyamma to deal with each visitor. Supporting the weak, consoling the afflicted, imparting courage to the frightened, and giving the hopeful message of the gospel to all were each part of Leyamma's mission work during the initial ten years of Mandiram. There were prayer meetings and Bible classes in Mandiram. There were special meetings for women from the local area. Leyamma also took a keen interest in the welfare of her coworkers. In addition to supervising their work, she gave guidance in their work. Any deficiencies in their attire or cleanliness were lovingly brought to their attention, and repeat offenders were warned or reprimanded in a loving way.

Leyamma always demanded an extreme degree of cleanliness in Mandiram, where over fifty patients resided. Regular sweeping and washing of the floors, burying the refuse, cleaning the drainage channels, and similar practices resulted in a clean atmosphere at Mandiram. This often brought compliments from the visitors. Her work extended outside the building too. Agriculture and poultry farming were promoted in Mandiram. Feeding her chicken and doves was a hobby Leyamma enjoyed.

She faced all difficult situations with courage and confidence. There once was a fire in the kitchen. The sevinee in the kitchen fainted and was on the floor. Leyamma put the fire out, emptying large pots of water over it, and then sprinkled cold water on the unconscious sevinee's face and woke her up.

Those fifty or more residents of Mandiram had rather undisciplined backgrounds. Bringing discipline to these people in their old age was a Herculean task that Leyamma had to face daily. There were instances where she was falsely accused of stealing things from residents. And sometimes residents stole things from

Mandiram and sold them outside. Fighting between residents was a regular feature, and Leyamma had to be the peacemaker at every fight. In another letter to a friend, Leyamma wrote, "Recently there was a fight between Kadamattam Ammumma and Pallippattu Ammumma. They often go on with wrestling matches too."

At the Zenith of Glory

June–July 1943 was a special period in the history of Mandiram and its co-founder, Leyamma. As mentioned earlier, support from the public for the new venture was phenomenal. Annual income that was only 556 rupees in the first year became 11,813 in the tenth year (1943). There was a donation of 2,500 rupees from an anonymous donor for building a better residence for the refugees. Someone gave 1,000 rupees toward the chapel building fund. Leyamma was ecstatic. In a letter to a friend, she wrote, "In every way The Lord is caring for His children. Often we get discouraged. Let us enjoy His presence each day and taste His love. Let us be diligent in prayer. Who can explain God's mysteries? Let this compound be filled with buildings, let thousands be healed of their infirmities and let those who die do it with dignity and in peace. Kindly continue to pray for renewed strength in our work."

Encouragement and support from every corner resulted in an increased workload. Sleepless nights and missed meals were common. Construction of the general ward was in progress. They wanted to complete the project by June when the dispensary was scheduled to be officially opened. About twenty laborers continued to work at night, and Leyamma was in charge of cooking and feeding them. Several youth volunteers also worked at night leveling the courtyard. They too needed coffee and snacks. Leyamma wrote to another friend about this period: "It is pretty busy here these days. The building construction is in progress. Carpenters, doctor, nurses, patients all keep us busy. Cooking, hospital visits, visiting the sick at home, going around begging for used clothes all takes every minute of the day and a good portion of the night too, giving us no time to rest and very little time to sleep. We are all pretty tired. Kunjoojamma is laid up with infected wound on her hand from washing a broken medicine bottle."

The Second World War was showing its worst effects by this time. Burma had fallen to the Japanese attack, and the steady flow of rice from Burma to India came to a sudden standstill. Even Sir C. P. Ramaswamy Iyer's statement in the Travancore assembly that "we will have to survive eating hay and grass" brought fear and concern to everyone's heart. To achieve an effective distribution of the crops to its people, the government of Travancore purchased the entire supply of crops directly from the farmers. All contributions the farmers normally would make to Mandiram also stopped because of this ordinance. Scarcity of rice made it hard to manage Mandiram. Leyamma wrote in a letter: "Yesterday there was no rice, we all ate tapioca and lentil. Everyone is in misery. Poor people get to eat some rice one in four or five days! Raggi and lentil help to fill the belly."

At least in Mandiram, they survived on tapioca, which was the main crop around the region. Large amounts of tapioca were bought; the sevinees cleaned and boiled them and dried them in the sun. Then the food was kept in storage. Leyamma was so busy with all this hard work; it really affected her health. Still, she did not want to take a break while her friends were working hard.

A letter she wrote on June 8, 1941, included this:

> Some of my girl friends addresses me "Mother Superior". Reading your letter made me laugh, even though I was on bed with severe backache. Nobody died after you left Mandiram, may be God knows that there is no one to carry the body to the grave! I have been getting this severe back pain for the past one week. I want to continue to work till I become too ill to work. Today I am writing letters to a few

of my friends. Unless I stop doing the laundry, my backache won't go away. We need someone to help us here. This year all 150 measures of raw rice were milled in the ural by me and my friends. In between we worked on tapioca, did laundry, cleaned the rooms and toilets, and did all the cooking. Please pray that we get adequate help to continue doing all the work in Mandiram. Me too have a wound on my toe and yesterday I had to read my bible in bed.

In another letter she wrote,

A one hundred year old woman from Omalloor died yesterday. As soon as we buried her another person died. Two deaths in a day! Rice is scarce. Even kerosine is rationed and its supply is steadily going down. We eat supper before sun goes down. Bible reading too is only during the day time. What can I say? This is what the whole world is going through, we too share the troubles with the rest.

The workload was steadily increasing. There were too many hungry souls to be fed, and the sevinees often had to go to bed hungry. Still, even in the midst of all these hardships, they had joy and peace. Leyamma went around singing. From the leadership position, she brought herself to the role of a servant. Like a young girl, she went around joking and singing. There was a special brightness in her face. Even her time for Bible reading and meditation was affected by the busyness at work. "I would like to sit under a tree and pray till my thirst for prayer is quenched," she once commented.

Her brother George, who was then the secretary for Mandiram, had to send away some who came seeking admission to Mandiram, because of a lack of resources and space. Leyamma never liked rejecting anyone. One afternoon, from her kitchen she saw an emaciated, elderly gentleman slowly approaching the office, with the aid of a cane. She sent someone ahead to talk to George, requesting that he not refuse admission to the old man. She said, "Who knows—this could be Jesus." That was her attitude to each person who came seeking help at Mandiram.

Leyamma was anxiously awaiting the arrival of God's kingdom on earth. George continued with his Bible study classes at Mandiram. Leyamma often missed her brother's classes because of her busy schedule. One week before her death, Leyamma commented, "Tonight I'm going for Kunjichayan's Bible study."

Her friends said, "We too are coming." And they all made it for that class.

Day-to-day running of the dispensary was the topic for discussion that night. Someone summarized the issue as follows:

> We should get funds. We should get doctor and other employees. We will serve the people of this area. As Christ did heal the sick so will we heal our sick neighbors. We are going to sell a thousand shares for the hospital at ten rupees a share and raise funds. We will divide the shares between three or five hundred households and ask them to support the dispensary by contributing every month to raise enough funds to pay the salary of the doctor and other employees. We will teach our people on health issues and also go to their homes and pray with them. In this way the physical and spiritual health of our villagers will be improved. In this way God's name will be glorified. Like the shepherds announced on the night of Jesus' birth there will be …"

At this point Leyamma, who had remained silent thus far, shouted out, "So, God's Kingdom is already here!" These were some of the last few words of faith from the lips of Leyamma. She was elated to see God's kingdom on earth!

June 4, 1942, was a Sunday. At four o'clock that afternoon, the dispensary was inaugurated. That was a day of great celebration at Mandiram. This was the first public meeting since the Mandiram had opened its doors ten years earlier. A new building for the Mandiram also was dedicated and opened on the same day. Mr. K. K. Lukose, BA, BL, presided over the meeting. He had arrived early in the afternoon and met with the sevinees and expressed his congratulations to Leyamma and the team for their exemplary work among the poor and needy. This was the first time her work was being publicly acknowledged and praised by dignitaries. All the hard work and all the sufferings that she endured in secrecy were now acknowledged in public. She was extremely happy and thankful. She was running around all over the place welcoming visitors and thanking each one. She did not forget to give a warning note to her friends, saying, "Please don't become proud by all these praises. The work that we did is nothing; tax collectors and adulterers will be entering the kingdom way before we do."

The week that followed was joyful and restful for Leyamma. She filled those days joking with friends, getting some time to sleep, and writing letters to several of her friends.

On July 14, 1943, she wrote to her brother, the Rev. P. C. Cheriyan:

Dear Achan,

Dedication of the dispensary went well. I can see patients standing outside and taking their medications. After you left us, four of the inmates died in Mandiram. Two are so sick that they may die any time. Collection of rice has drastically dropped. There is some paddy in stock, we have tapioca in store. Our inmates had something to eat for every meal so far. With one more office to care for (dispensary) Kunjichayan is keeping very busy.

There is talk about cholera all around. They have started inoculating all school children. I heard that a few fainted after the cholera shot at M. T. Seminary School.

We are working hard with very little rest. Always there will be three or four nearing death at Mandiram.

Your

Pennamma.

Another letter of July 13, 1943, from Leyamma goes like this:

Dear ———,

In spite of the scarcity of rice in the market, we never had to miss a meal for our inmates so far, thanks be to God. A full day's work does not fetch a measure of rice for the laborer. We too share the suffering with the rest of the world. God has been leading Mandiram for the past ten years wonderfully well.

Someone donated money for buying medicine. Please continue to pray for the dispensary which is a blessing to the public as well as the inmates.

As of today, One hundred and forty inmates died in Mandiram. Kindly excuse my inability to write to you more often; there is scarcity for paper and postage stamps too. Even from your station in a foreign land you can continue to pray for us. We would love to learn about your situation too. Do you get enough rice? Or are you eating wheat and grass? Tapioca keeps us going here in Travancore. With the news of wars and unrest I feel that the

second coming of The Lord is at hand. Let us stay
prepared.

Sincerely yours,
Pennamma.

The news about a cholera epidemic was the main item in the
newspapers. Everywhere there was the talk of "death."

Leyamma celebrated her thirty-first birthday by attending
Holy Communion along with her friends. After they returned to
Mandiram, there was another prayer and praise session with friends.
One of them put a garland on Leyamma's neck. She commented,
"The Lord who kept me going this far is a good God. My dear mom
died at the age of thirty-two. I don't think that I will make it to
thirty-two."

On another occasion Leyamma said to her friends: "Guess who
among us is going to die first! If I die first you can all divide my
property: my umbrella [she didn't have one], my Bible, and my
suitcase. Kunjoojamma should sit by me and sing. None of you
should cry. You should all together bathe me. I should wear a simple
plain white attire, just like any other inmate who dies in Mandiram.
There should be two candles on the head end, and none at the
foot end. And my burial should be just like any other inmate of
Mandiram."

No one knows why she prayed like this on that Wednesday
night: "God, let me die a martyr's death in your battlefield. If I am
an obstacle to the smooth functioning of your Mandiram, please
uproot me from here."

When discussions on buying new clothes or starting a new
project came, Leyamma would say, "Let this cholera epidemic be
over."

Youth volunteers cooperated with the public health officials to
give cholera immunizations to all in the neighborhood. At Mandiram
there were at least five bedridden with diarrhea. Leyamma and
friends attended to these men in isolation in private rooms. Some

died. One gentleman who came to Mandiram complaining of severe cramping and diarrhea died soon; later on they found out that he came from an area where cholera was prevalent. He also was buried, and two more days went by.

That Saturday was a special day at the local Mar Thoma Church. Bishop Mathews Mar Athanacious had been visiting the church and staying there for the night. He was a close family friend of Leyamma. While working at Keezhillam as a teacher, the bishop had close association with George and Leyamma's brother Kochayan (the Rev. P. C. Cheriyan) and had been a visitor at their home often. There was a meeting of the women's association of the church that Saturday morning, and the bishop presided over the meeting. Leyamma made a lengthy speech on the work of *sevikasanghom* and its effective mission in church.

When the bishop visited Mandiram, Leyamma, along with George, took the bishop around and showed the facility to this leader of the church. She talked to the bishop in detail on the working of the recently opened dispensary.

Leyamma returned to her room. Her clothes that had been washed that morning were still on the clothesline. She pulled them off, ironed them, and set them aside to wear to church in the morning. All the clothes for George, too, had been in her suitcase for all these years. She took them out, gave them to Sevinee Annamma, and said, "Now on keep all these in your suitcase; now on you are in charge of Kunjichayan." And she closed her box.

Leyamma went to bed, ready to get up on Sunday morning and go for the Holy Communion service at the church.

Leyamma felt extremely weak and tired that night. Twice she had diarrhea.

Though feeling tired, she combed her hair and changed into her clothes to go to church. She had another episode of diarrhea. "Never knew I had this much of water in my belly!" she exclaimed. While getting ready to go to church, there was more diarrhea, and she decided against going to church. Quite disappointed, she told her friends: "I'm staying back; you may go ahead."

Sitting on her cot, Leyamma was listening to the service in the church. With her head covered with a piece of cloth, she participated in the entire service, responding as much as she could. Some of her friends who were checking on her in between were relieved to see that she was attending the service from her room.

Leyamma's absence at the Communion service was obvious to her friends. They all came to her room right after the service. Leyamma was very weak and not responding well at all. They called George, and he found her body cold and her eyes sunken and closed. But she was still alive.

Immediately a nurse and a local ayurvedic doctor were sent for. Under their care, Leyamma got better, opened her eyes, and stood up. She was ashamed of having created all this fuss! She took a little porridge, and everyone left.

By about four in the afternoon, Leyamma had severe diarrhea and she collapsed. Her body was ice cold. George wasted no time. He sent for the doctor at the district hospital of Kottayam. Dr. Achy Iype arrived within twenty minutes. One could see that the situation was very serious from the expression on the doctor's face. After giving a couple of injections to Leyamma, the doctor took her in her car and drove to Kottayam. There were enough people to help at the hospital. Doctors were waiting for her. Dr. Iype, being a regular visitor to Mandiram, knew Leyamma and George very well. She was a close friend of Mandiram too. She did all she could to help her friend and the founder of Mandiram.

At midnight, there was no sign of improvement. By then the crowd at the hospital was huge. "Who will give some blood for Leyamma?" Dr. Iype asked the crowd. There were so many who wanted to donate blood that night in an attempt to save their dear friend Leyamma. After the testing of several people, blood was taken from Leyamma's cousin Chackochy, who said, "Take as much as you want—I want Leyamma to live, even if I die."

After the blood transfusion, there was a glimmer of hope, but it did not last long. Leyamma, the lady who had attended to 153 people on their deathbeds in Mandiram, was being attended to now by all those friends from Mandiram and the vicinity. The one who helped to quench the thirst of all those who died in her presence was now begging for a drop of water. She was asking, "Kunjichayan, Kochayan, Chackochychaya, Kunjumon, Kuttacha ... please give me some water." But her thirst was never quenched. She felt a sense of peace and said, "I feel better now." At 2:45 a.m., Leyamma opened her eyes, looked up as if fixing her eyes on someone's eyes there, and breathed her last.

Along with the sevinees in Mandiram, Leyamma had been there to massage the eyes closed for 153 destitute persons, and now as the 154th inmate, her eyes were massaged and closed by her friends. She had been there to quench the thirst of the dying residents at Mandiram, and ultimately she had become the one begging for water. Finally, she had moved to the presence of her Lord and Savior, praising and adoring Him along with the multitude of angels in heaven. It had been her desire to sit and pray to her satisfaction; now she can look at the face of her Savior and stay there as long as she pleases. She had washed and ironed her clothes in preparation to go to the Communion service at church that Sunday, but only hours later she would go on her final journey into the presence of her Lord and Savior. During her life she was serving women and men, and now she has been promoted to serve God at His feet.

sevinees in Mandiram 1976

Cousin Chackochy, who donated blood to Leyamma

CHAPTER 5

The Memory of a Righteous One Lasts Forever

*A*nother one of my trips to India had a special purpose: to interview a few people who had close association with Mr. P. C. George. Among them, the foremost was his nephew and namesake, my eldest brother-in-law, Mr. George Cheriyan, whom relatives have often referred to as Georgekutty. He is a retired chief engineer of the Kerala State Electricity Board, Trivandrum. His childhood memories of Valiyappachan, as he calls P. C. George, were still fresh and very much alive in his mind. For him there is no doubt that Valiyappachan was the person who has influenced him the most.

There are two letters from Valiyappachan that were written to this nephew at age ten that he still keeps as valuable treasures. Four sheets of papers with handwritten notes on both sides have been fading in color and torn at their folds. They were taken out from among his most important documents and placed on the dining table so I could take a few snapshots. Gently I unfolded them and read the contents. Each of the sentences in those four pages was carefully and skillfully written by someone who was extremely busy with his job, his passionate work among the youth, and his social and spiritual activities, all the while taking care of his three orphaned younger siblings. A loving and caring uncle who found time to write in such detail to his oldest nephew—it sure put me to shame as I reflected on my falling short in communicating with the youngsters in my life. Both of the letters showed me the personality of P. C. George.

The opening line of the first letter of P. C. George made reference to my wife and his niece, Leyamma. He said, "As I am writing this letter little Leyamma is running around in the house. She acts shy to come to me and hides behind the doors when I call her."

Then there were precious pieces of advice to the young nephew in the letter. Valiyappachan wanted to develop Georgekutty's interest in reading and improving penmanship by writing. Valiyappachan recounted a personal example of how he had enjoyed writing one hundred pages to please his grade-school teacher who had assigned him to write thirty pages during the school holidays. It was captivating to see him describe how the rest of his classmates showed up with fewer pages or none at all. They all had excuses like "was sick, lost the paper, it rained on the paper, the dog ate the homework."

He congratulated his nephew on his magnanimity in giving his new umbrella to an adopted sister, Kamala. Georgekutty was asked to treat Kamala as his own sister, which he did.

There were instructions for developing reading habits and better study habits as well. Valiyappachan was the reason for the voracious appetite for reading that George Cheriyan ultimately developed, he admitted to me. When he, Georgekutty, graduated from fifth grade at the top of his class, he became the winner of a new Bible. Three rupees were given to him to buy a Bible, and he gave the money to Valiyappachan to obtain a Bible in Kottayam. One day Georgekutty accompanied Valiyappachan to Kottayam to a book store whose owner was a family friend. There Valiyappachan picked five books for Georgekutty and made a special arrangement with the store owner. Georgekutty could take home, read, and return the books in as-new condition, while the three rupees would be kept as a deposit for the store owner. Under this arrangement, Georgekutty soon read all the books in the store without spending any money! At the end, Valiyappachan bought a new Bible with the money and presented it to Georgekutty, who was an avid reader by then.

Valiyappachan had very little exposure to English in school. But he knew that many of the treasures in history, theology, and literature were in English. This made him desire to study English on his own. George Cherian mentioned to me how Valiyappachan sought the help of the three sisters of a boy named Thankakuttan in learning to read English. After school, P. C. George would go to their home and read the books in their presence, asking them for help in proper pronunciation and usage. His interest in reading was so profound that by the time he finally got access to English-language books of the famous authors, he made it a point to read them from cover to cover. A translated edition of *Les Misérables* was among the books that touched him and influenced him.

"Learn, Reform, and Transform" was P. C. George's motto. For him, learning was the cornerstone for reformation as well as transformation. As a model teacher, he influenced several generations of students in school. As a social reformer, his influence spread over differing socioeconomic and religious groups and all age groups. George's fight against social evils such as untouchability and the caste system hit the core of the society. He mobilized the youth against social evils such as alcoholism. His hard work to educate the general public regarding basic health care and public health went a long way in preventing widespread epidemics of infectious diseases. George took it upon himself to go from house to house in times of epidemics to collect detailed data on the number of cases and the modes of transmission in the community. He sought help from the authorities to get immunization of the villagers, and he educated the villagers as to the need for adequate immunizations.

Cooperative banking was another area of interest for George. As mentioned earlier, most of the villagers were able to carry on from day to day. But in times of medical or social emergency, they often lacked funds and went into deep debt by borrowing money at high interest rates. By getting enough villagers to take membership in the cooperative society, George and his friends organized the first-ever cooperative bank in Mundakapadam.

After teaching in the Puthuppally school for a few years, George was transferred to a government training school at Kottayam. This gave him the opportunity to attend many of the meetings at Kottayam and to get to know more people in different arenas in society. Full-time teaching, along with the activities of Mandiram, prayer meetings, Bible studies, and the other social reform activities kept him extremely busy.

It was at this time that he got a transfer to Perumbavoor with a promotion. He was in a dilemma. Should he accept the transfer or should he resign the job and go full time with the other activities? It was not an easy decision. He needed the income to continue supporting his siblings' education and providing for the day-to-day expenses at home. His health was failing too. He decided to join the service at Perumbavoor. He took a short leave to settle things at Mandiram. Then he started work at the new place.

Soon, however, George resigned from that job, from the occupation he loved and performed with utmost loyalty, in order to fully devote his efforts to Mandiram and his other community activities. Even after resigning his full-time job, George did not have enough hours in his days to complete his chores. Opening the dispensary and taking the initial bold steps for a new hospital were no easy matters. Finding enough qualified and dedicated men and women to staff the organization was also a Herculean task. Yet George carried out his mission faithfully and ran the race well. While he lived only to age fifty-one, he accomplished more than anyone could in a long life span.

P. C. George and His Love for Children

P. C. George, a man of great wisdom, who was always busy with major projects, still had the heart of a child, and he found time to be with children. Though he remained unmarried for life by choice, he shared his love lavishly among his nephews, nieces, and a few children in Mandiram. I was lucky enough to get to know several of them. Marykutty, Kamalam, and Ponnamma are among them. Valsalan was another whom I never met.

Janaki was a woman from North Paravoor and made her livelihood begging in the streets of Kottayam. When she became sick with nobody to care for her, she and her four-year-old daughter came to Mandiram. Soon Janaki breathed her last, leaving her daughter to the care of Mandiram authorities. Sevinees took care of Marykutty, who had her schooling at the Buchanan School at Pallom and Bethel Asramam School, in Varikkad. Then she returned to Mandiram, where she is still serving as one of the sevinees.

Another young girl, Kamalam, came with her mom to Mandiram in destitute condition. Her mom, too, died while in Mandiram. Kamalam, known as Kamalakshi, stayed with the sevinees and had her first five years of schooling there. Later on, she moved to Keezhillam and attended Saint Thomas High School while staying with the Rev. P. C. Cheriyan and family—including my wife and her siblings. After graduating from there, Kamalam returned to Mandiram and served at the operating room in the hospital for many years. She is retired and resides in Mandiram.

In another instance, an elderly gentleman belonging to the Nair caste came to Mandiram holding the hand of his young daughter and requested shelter. P. C. George responded, "Our policy is not to take children as inmates in Mandiram. If you can find placement for your daughter elsewhere and come, then you can stay here."

"I will have no life apart from my dear daughter" was the reply from the father. That dad's love made George change his mind, and he admitted them both to Mandiram.

The daughter stayed with the sevinees. At daybreak, the father would be at the doorstep of the residence of the sevinees looking for his dear daughter, Ponnamma.

Soon he too died, and Ponnamma was left with the sevinees. After her first four years of schooling in Manganam, she was sent to Miss Baker School in Kottayam, and eventually she graduated from high school.

Ponnamma pursued her nursing training in Kolar, returned to Mandiram, and worked in the hospital there for a short period. She migrated to the United States and settled in Chicago and raised a family. She retired in Arizona from her long nursing career and passed away in 2010. My wife and I visited Ponnamma in Chicago as well as in Arizona. Spending time with her and her beautiful family made us witness God's miraculous transformation of an orphan through the work of another orphan, P. C. George!

Valsalan was another youngster who was brought to Mandiram in very poor health. There he was nursed to good health and became a favorite kid for the older gentlemen. When P. C. George fell ill, Valsalan was ready to take his place and die if that would make his George Sir better.

After the interview with George Cherian, I had no trouble understanding why he, Georgekutty, had become so pivotal in shaping the future of his own younger siblings—he simply followed the example of a great uncle!

Chapter 6

Letters from P. C. George

P. C. George lived at a time when communication was mainly through in-person conversation or through letters. Being always busy with many projects, George could not be everywhere to talk to all. He maintained his contact with his friends and students in his Bible study through letters. In doing so, he was following in the footsteps of Saint Paul, who spread his message to the believers in Corinth, Rome, and Ephesus via letters. Many of George's letters were a source of encouragement, and many were consolation for those who were in trouble.

A good friend of George passed away after a short illness. Before his death, he had encouraged his wife to go for mission training at Vanitha Mandiram in Tiruvalla. Gorge wrote the following letter to this woman:

Dear sister,

I regret my inability to travel that far this time. I know it is impossible to convey everything through a letter. Hope to visit you without much delay. I believe that God has a great plan for your life, and I want you to realize that. The baby chick coming out of an eggshell thinks that his world under the wings of the mother hen is very wide. Soon it will be kept under a larger shelter made for him by the owner. Afterward, it will be released to the yard where for the first time it experiences the beauty and the enormity of the sky and the surroundings. Like the baby chick, you spent ten months in your mother's womb. You had a few years at your husband's home. Now you are away from both those houses which God tore apart and put you in a new home to train you for building the eternal heavenly home. Please don't think for a moment that tearing your home, here was an unkind act of God. I want you to see it as God's mercy. After a couple of years of training at the Vanitha Mandiram, I want you to go to the place where God sends you and work for Him. Your husband did work with vigor for the kingdom of God. Please don't try to rebuild the home that God tore apart. I want you to fly up into the new sky, where God has great plans for you. When you get some time, please come and stay with us for a week; Christian fellowship gives you the strength to go on.

Another letter that he wrote to a prospective sevinee to Mandiram includes the following:

You may be asked to join us shortly. Come prepared to be the door mat for everyone to step on, to be sacrificial in God's work and die little by little daily bearing the cross. We have a large cross painted on the floor of our portico; that is our motto. Pour out the blood of your youth in drops for the native youth. Are you ready to give up your present job that gives you four to five hundred rupees per month and a bright future for a service that may assure you just porridge every day? Do it only if you have the divine calling.

And there were several in the community who gave up drinking alcohol. He wrote the following letter to one who was saved from alcohol addiction:

Dear Brother,

Heard that you gave up drinking a fortnight back. I'm very happy and am praising God for the news. Why dint you let us also know of this news earlier as we rejoice with you more than anyone else. God has bestowed his grace upon you and your family. Let Him sustain you with the heavenly manna.

Make sure you give up all your old company and find new friends who do not drink. I can assure you that all my friends are your friends too.

I would like come to meet you in person and talk to you soon. Ensure you my prayers for you every day.

See you soon.

P. C. George.
Sincerely, P. C. George.

CHAPTER 7

P. C. George and Bible Study Classes

George was a student of the Bible all through his life. His knowledge of the Old Testament and the New Testament was deep. The teacher in him came alive in every class he gave for any age group. He made the classes interesting for anyone who attended. "Learn, teach, and transform" was his philosophy. He took pains to attend Bible classes by walking several miles a day during his busy career as a student and then as a teacher. He imparted this knowledge to many youngsters in the community, which led to transformation in their lives. This resulted in many of them following him in his work among the poor and the destitute. He conducted classes for different age groups on various days of the week. Physical ailments and busy schedules never could hinder his resolve in continuing with the classes.

He prepared each lesson with the seriousness of a schoolteacher who makes daily lessons for the class. He always had the notes as well as the materials to help in the teaching. Often he explained the Bible stories by showing a map of Palestine and the surrounding region. This helped his students to get a better idea about the places where Christ performed the miracles and where Saint Paul traveled on his mission trips.

George talked about the Christian home in his classes. He stressed the need for Christian love among members of the family. The family of Mary, Martha, and Lazarus at Bethany was his example of a loving family.

In his classes for women, George taught his students on subjects such as cleanliness, child care, and home economics. Some of these women compiled their notes and published a book in Malayalam titled *Graha Lekshmi*.

The necessity of prayer was always stressed in these classes. Once George commented that twenty-four hours a day were not enough for his prayer life. The present-day Mandiram Hospital and the other important institutions of Mandiram stand in the formerly deserted place where George, either alone or with his friends, spent hours in prayer shedding tears.

Nadukkottil Kunjachan, Fr. C. C. Korah, and Vazhavelil V. J. Joseph were some of his prayer partners over these hills and deserted places.

George even started a special study class for boys who were home for midsummer vacation. Instead of wasting their time sleeping and watching movies, these youths were given another option for study and other joint activities.

CHAPTER 8

George: The Model Teacher

"*I* can trace all the growth in my life to the teaching vocation that was given to me," George once stated. He considered it a noble profession and made it part of his gospel work. He was constantly aware of a teacher's role in transforming the future generation, and he took it very seriously. His aim was not merely to have his students learn the textbooks and pass the examination; his classes often included advice and guidance for betterment of their future.

It was Francis Bacon who said, "Reading makes a man perfect." George cultivated a reading habit from early childhood, and it grew as he grew up. This helped him to develop his knowledge in different subjects, enabling him to be effective in his teaching of Sunday school classes as well as in his sermons, Bible studies, prayer meetings, and various social reform activities.

His interest in education was intense, and he wanted to impart the best possible education to all his siblings.

The salary of a schoolteacher in those days was only ten rupees a month, and George used it economically to educate his siblings and to meet the daily necessities at home. It is amazing that George had enough funds to help those in need. When he met the orphans, he would tell them, "Once I and my siblings were in the same situation as you are now. We lost our parents when we were small children. God, who wonderfully took care of us, will take care of you also."

All four siblings together carried out the household duties. They had to cook early in the morning before going to school. Often George would not have any lunch. Sometimes, he would spend one *chakram* (a small coin) for his lunch.

Leyamma took over the kitchen at an early age, and that was a great consolation for the brothers. She would cook and often be late for school, even on days of examination. In spite of repeated attempts, Leyamma could not pass the final examination in seventh grade.

George was a student for life. After becoming a teacher, he privately enrolled in the Malayalam Vidwan course and passed the examination. During his summer vacations, he performed mission work.

As a model teacher, George became the favorite for a many a student all around central Travancore. Corporal punishment was something George rarely resorted to. One of his students at the Puthuppally school has stated, "I was caned by George Sir on the palm once for telling lie in class, and that punishment transformed my life. And that helped me not to lie in the future."

George was never late for a class, and he never taught a class without adequately preparing. His generosity led him to buy textbooks for those of his students who could not afford to buy their own. He often visited homes of his students too.

Eventually he was sent to Changanacherry for higher training, and he had to walk ten miles each way every day! After finishing the training, George was posted to Kottayam V. H. School. Even though he had to walk four miles each way, his job at Kottayam led him to get to know several men who were of tremendous influence in his life. One was Mr. K. K. Kuruvilla, a teacher at M. T. Seminary School, who was a prominent educator, Bible teacher, and social reformer. Gorge enjoyed the time he could spend with him.

Ravindranatha Tagore, a philosopher and poet of India, Mohandas Kramchand Gandhi, the father of modern India, and C. F. Andrews, a writer and missionary, were among the dignitaries who visited and spent time at the home of Kuruvilla. George utilized these days to get to know these great personalities and listen to their speeches and admonitions.

It was Kuruvilla who stated, "The churches in India are debating over issues of worship and faith while wasting their time and talents and forgetting the Lord's commandments. It is high time for the church to wake up and carry out His commandments." George was motivated, and we should be too!

CHAPTER 9

A Model Family

*I*t is said that people can choose their friends but cannot choose their family. George was fortunate to be born into a God-fearing family. During the very few short years in which he had his parents and grandparents with him, he received valuable training and guidance from them. As previously noted, he lost his mother when he was in fourth grade and his father when he was only fifteen years old.

In his journal, George wrote about life at home with his sister and brothers. He stated, "We, siblings at home was a fellowship. We prayed with each other, worked together and nothing was done without discussing with all the four. Once I told my siblings, 'Being the eldest in the family makes me responsible for bringing marriage proposals for each of you. Nevertheless, I want each of you to carefully consider and choose your spouses.' Though I repeatedly told them this, both my brothers put that responsibility on my shoulders."

George also recalled as follows: "Chackochy got married first, and the membership in our family grew to five. There was always harmony in our home. Second brother Kochu Kochu (P. C. Cheriyan) was called to the priesthood in Mar Thomas Church. We all spent time together and in prayer before deciding in favor of the calling. He too had several marriage proposals. We wanted someone with vision, dedication and sacrificial life to be his partner for life. It was Leyamma who proposed the name of a young lady who was with her at Vanitha Mandiram as the bride for her brother. Kunjamma, Leyamma's friend, was from a prominent Christian family, was educated and had Christian training. Everyone agreed, and our number in the family grew to six. Bringing in two women from outside into our home did not make our bond lighter but tighter still."

The Rev. P. C. Cheriyan was the principal of Saint Thomas High School, Keezhillam, for three and a half decades. He was instrumental in bringing the school to prominence. During this period, in his clergy role in the Mar Thoma Church, he was responsible for several parishes in the area also. He passed away in 1978.

The other brother, Chackochy, taught at Keezhillam Mar Thomas Primary School for many years and passed away in 1951.

The majority of the residents of Mandiram came from broken homes. Observing this, George, in his classes and Bible studies, stressed the need to strengthen the family unit.

George and Leyamma dedicated their whole lives for the service of the poor, and each decided to remain unmarried for life.

The Cooperative Society and Reformation of the Village

Reforming the village was the basic step in developing the country, according to P. C. George. He had the maturity to see persons of every class as the same before the Creator. George's greatest wealth was a group of friends willing to make any sacrifice with him. These men regularly met at George's home, discussing the needs of the villagers and the best way to spread the gospel among them.

As the first step, they selected three hundred homes in the village and started their village reformation activities. Along with his friends, George visited all those homes and conducted a survey, probably the first of its kind in India. They collected data on the villagers' state of health, education, economic status, major problems they faced in life, and many more issues like these. This team firmly believed that unless the economic status of the villagers was improved, no reform was going to be effective.

Many charts and posters were made, based on the findings of this survey. George and his friends conducted meetings at public places and roadsides, showing these charts. This made the public more aware of their need for improving cleanliness and public health. George and his friends also spoke about the ill effects of alcohol abuse.

Mr. K. K. Kuruvilla, who had seen the cooperative societies in action in Holland and Denmark, was always there to advise them in the formative years. Cooperative societies were unheard of in Kerala before this time. George, far ahead of his time in wisdom and planning, could foresee the society helping to raise some village members out of poverty.

The first cooperative society was thus opened at Manganam. From a small beginning, it soon grew to be a large organization. It was in 1931 that its first store was opened in Manganam. There were only ten members, each with a share at ten rupees, and the capital was just one hundred rupees. In short few years, the share value went up to two hundred rupees and the membership grew to four hundred!

Poverty had a strong grip on the villagers during this period. A full day's work by a laborer fetched him a measure of rice that was just enough to feed his family. Illness in the family, needed repairs on the house, marriage of girls, and other occurrences requiring extra funds threw the villagers into deep debt. The cooperative society was the solution in these situations. Some ladies got funds to buy a cow. Other villagers got a loan at a low interest rate. All in all, the society helped to reform the village.

George served as the secretary of the cooperative society in the initial few years and then as its president for another short while. His plan of management was based on keeping the Bible in one hand and the account book in the other. As George believed fully that God's kingdom would be completed only through economically upgrading the poor, he deemed any time spent on the cooperative society to be time well invested. He instructed his followers to trust each other, trust in themselves, and above all trust God. George rightly foresaw the cooperative society securing better employment, education, health care, and banking, as well as small industries.

Chapter 10

Letters from P. C. George

There are not many letters from Mr. P. C. George that are still available. A few personal letters that he sent to his nephew George Cheriyan are treasured and in his safekeeping. I had the opportunity to review them and make copies of two of these letters. One that is displayed elsewhere in this book was addressed to George Cheriyan (Georgekutty) and two nieces, Molly and Susy. The letter opens with a reference to a little girl, Leyamma, as she runs around in the house in P. C. George's presence, studying and observing her Valyappachan from a safe distance. This third niece, Leyamma, who is my wife, was only three years old then and was staying at Mandiram, away from her parents and siblings.

P. C. George, while being busy with all the activities and projects around him, still found time to keep his contact with the young nephew and nieces through letters. His love for the little ones is evident from the start to the finish of these handwritten letters. He was aware of child psychology and gave reassurance to the five-year-old Susy that his love for her had not diminished a bit just because Leyamma was there close to him! In the letter, he was eager to know if Susy's physical ailments were all gone. And he left an open invitation for any of them to come to Manganam for the Christmas vacation.

Letters from people who love us and care for us are to be treasured. They give us joy and comfort as we go back to read and reread them. With the development of the satellite communication systems and improvements in telecommunications with texting, faxing, tweeting, and FaceTiming, the practice of letter writing became a lost art. Unfortunately, none of these modern forms of communication gives me the distinctive feeling that a handwritten letter gives. A letter is a permanent document that is tangible and talks to my senses in special ways that a phone call can never do. As I go back and reread a letter, often I find new meaning and ideas that I missed the first time. How I wish I wrote more letters to the younger generation in my life! I still enjoy getting a handwritten letter. P. C. George was very regular in letter writing.

CHAPTER 11

Great Minds Think Alike

It was in 1939 that P. C. George chanced to meet Toyohiko Kagawa, the world-renowned missionary from Kobe, Japan. George was one of the delegates in the global conference of missionaries at Thambaram in the state of Madras. There, George got to know the great missionary pioneer from Japan; soon the younger missionary was attracted to the great vision and practical approach of Kagawa to the practice of Christianity.

Like George, Kagawa had been an orphan from his early childhood. He had been sent away to school, which was when two American missionary teachers, Harry W. Mayers and Charles A. Logan, took him into their homes. After learning English from these missionaries, Kagawa converted to Christianity and was disowned by his remaining extended family. After studying in Kobe Theological Seminary, he enrolled in Princeton Theological Seminary for two years (1914–1916). He believed that Christianity in action was the truth of Christian doctrine and was troubled by the seminarians' concern for technicalities of doctrine. In Japan, he was arrested more than once for his part in labor activism during strikes.

He worked hard to evangelize Japan's poor and to advocate for a peaceful foreign policy. In 1909, Kagawa moved into a Kobe slum with the intention of acting as a missionary sociologist.

He introduced the principle of "three-dimensional forestry" to persuade many of Japan's upland farmers to find a solution to soil erosion by widespread tree planting. He promoted the planting of fruit and nut trees that would achieve three benefits: provision of food for humans, provision of fodder for animals, and prevention of soil erosion.

George's vision was not much different from those of Kagawa. Like Kagawa, George was a missionary for the poor. He, too, believed in Christianity in action as the truth of Christian doctrine. Social reforms and social uplift of the downtrodden were on the agenda for both. George was never arrested for standing up for his beliefs, but he was always bold to speak the truth.

Kagawa influenced George in his future path. Another person who was an influence in George's life was Mohandas Karamchand Gandhi, the father of modern India. Gandhiji was a visionary who fought against the caste system and stood to uplift the status of the "untouchables" in society.

God sends the right persons in our path to guide us and direct us to achieve His purpose in our lives.

CHAPTER 12

The Candle Finally Burns Out!

P. C. George accomplished more great things in his short span of life than ten people could in that time. Laziness was not in his dictionary. He never thought of taking rest. Continuous activity was his lifestyle. He exemplified the motto "By faith we live." He truly believed and proved through his activities the statement that those who cannot love the brother whom they can see will not be able to love God whom they cannot see.

Continuous hard work with no rest took a toll on his health. Fighting against alcoholism in the community required much time and effort from him. The monsoon season did not help his arthritis either. Soon he experienced weakness in his left leg and left arm. Friends urged him to seek ayurvedic treatment and rest. He eventually agreed to take an herbal concoction prescribed by the Vayaskara ayurvedic physicians. Forty-eight doses of the medication did very little to improve his condition. Pain in his left arm was getting to be unbearable and he needed help to make even a small move.

In his diary there is a notation about this period of illness: "I have not read anything these days. Body has lost the stamina to read. Even opening and closing the eyelids is a chore. My left arm seems to be lifeless. Fortunately right arm is fine. This bed rest tags was imposed on me has helped me to meditate on so many things. Thankfulness to life's memories is a rare treasure indeed. As poor as I am, I feel more thankful and happy than the richest. Though poor on world's standards, I feel extremely rich in Godly affairs. I take pride in being called to serve the poor."

Among the many visitors that George had during his illness were Mr. Sreedharan, who was the first one from the Ezhava caste to earn a bachelor of arts degree, and Mr. V. J. Joseph, from another poor caste, who also graduated with a BA degree. These well-educated and well-disciplined young men were representing two poor castes in the area. It was an opportunity for George to share his experience growing up as a poor orphan and persevering to live a moral and fulfilling life. George hoped that his sharing this experience would help these young men to lead their own communities to a better future. George was living above the caste and religious boundaries. He could see everyone as his own brothers and sisters.

Even the illness could not rob George of his determination to continue with his work. Eventually he left his sickbed. It was during this period that he organized a fellowship of a few of the clergy and several of his friends around Manganam. Once he commented, "If God assess me not on my achievements, but on my attempts at all the opportunities given to me, then I am sure, I will get high marks."

He assembled fifty college students from the area and instructed them on the need for motivation and a proper aim in life. In August of 1951, his talk at a leadership conference of the Mar Thoma Church was on Christian life and practical life. He encouraged the audience to be truthful, genuine, and of high moral character in witnessing as Christians. Two days later he spoke in another antialcohol meeting in Puthuppally, addressing a large number of students. On August 15 there was another meeting celebrating the Independence Day of India. George was the chief speaker for that meeting too.

September 12, 1951, was the day they celebrated "Onam." A large meeting was planned for that day. Though George wanted to speak in that meeting at Puthuppally, he was found to be too weak. He sat on a chair next to the presiding officer and observed the whole thing with much enthusiasm. By the end of the meeting, George was too weak to walk. He was carried to a jeep and was driven to Mandiram.

He asked for a drink and received cumin water from the sevinees. To one he said, "Annamma, I have accomplished all that I wanted. It was my vision to see the leaders of differing denominations on a single platform. It happened today at Puthuppally; now I can die happy."

To his friends around him he said, "I am swimming in happiness, thinking of the thousands of people who love me. I have finished my race. I want to love and to be loved."

George was asked to take complete rest. For a few days he was moved to the home of Mr. K. K. Kurian, Kalarikkal, Manganam. George had full rest and proper food during those few days. As he was getting worse, he was brought back to Mandiram. Many people visited him during those days.

It was the night before George's demise. All of the sevinees and a few friends had gathered around his bed. George wanted them to go to sleep, telling them that he was alright. He called Mr. K. M. Thomas, Kizhakkeparambil, and entrusted the care of the sevinees to him. Then he called Sevinee Annamma and asked, "When Leyamma died it was the one hundred fifty-fourth death in Mandiram. How many destitute have died so far?" This brought tears to their eyes and nobody dared to answer.

When he insisted, Annamma whispered, "Three hundred fifty-one."

"Make sure that you write on my coffin, that I am the three hundred fifty-second destitute." That was his final instruction.

He continued to direct his close friends to carry on with his vision and mission. One time he said, "I know that the hospital and the Mandiram will go on, but I am not so sure about the antialcohol movement."

By the evening of September 27, George was getting very tired and weak. By the afternoon of September 29, his body was sweating, but his face became brighter and he was ready to leave this world. Friends around him started singing his favorite hymn: "*Aswasame yenikere thingeedunnu, viswasa kkannal njan nokkeedumbol.*"

The Rev. M. G. Chandy, who later on became Alexander Marthoma Metropolitan, did the prayer of dedication, and George said amen at the end. At about six o'clock in the evening, that noble spirit left its earthly abode. The candle that brought light into the darkness finally burned out!

The funeral was on September 30. A huge crowd was there for the funeral procession. People of differing faiths and beliefs had assembled to have a final glimpse of their dear friend and mentor. Juhanon Marthoma Metropolitan officiated at the funeral service. Mr. M. Iype gave the eulogy. The body was then buried beside the resting place of his dear sister Leyamma. Destitute Number 352 and Number 154 from Mandiram finally rested next to each other, awaiting the day of their resurrection!

CHAPTER 13

The Rev. P. C. Cheriyan and P. C. Chacko

*K*ochu Kochu, one of the brothers of P. C. George, looked up to George for guidance and direction. George wanted his younger siblings to get all the education they could. With the meager income of ten rupees per month as a primary-school teacher, George managed to provide for their education, all the while taking care of the day-to-day needs of the family.

All four siblings shared in running their home. George was the provider and guide. Everyone played his or her part in cooking, cleaning, washing, and praying. All decisions were made with the full consent and knowledge of all the four. Even the youngest among them, Leyamma, was asked at times to "preside over" their family meetings. Life lessons that they learned at home were invaluable for all of them. Caring for the poor, helping those in need, praising God in all circumstances, loving the Word of God, and loving their neighbors were important lessons that they learned from their parents and in turn practiced in their own lives.

As we have already seen, George decided to stay unmarried, devoting his whole life for the service of the less fortunate in the society. His sister Leyamma, too, stayed single and helped the elder brother in his humanitarian services. She took upon herself the responsibility of running Mandiram.

Kochu Kochu was the first college graduate in the Puthuparambil family. He was always aware of the wholehearted support from his siblings who helped him to achieve this. Soon he was appointed teacher at Puthuppally High School, very close to their home. This was welcome news to the whole family—another source of income to a family in financial need!

It was at this time that the Mar Thoma Church got approval from the government to start a high school in Perumbavoor. Mr. C. T. Mathew, the future Bishop Mathews Mar Athanaseus, was transferred from his post in Keezhillam Middle School to take charge in Perumbavoor. The church was looking for the right person to be the headmaster at the school. P. C. George found that person in his younger brother Kochu Kochu, who would resign his newly found job at Puthuppally and move to Keezhillam.

The Rev. E. J. George, a senior pastor in Mar Thoma Church and a close family friend of the Puthuparambil family, has recounted a conversation between the two brothers as follows:

P. C. GEORGE: "Kochu Kochu, your present job so close by is a blessing indeed. Now you are a teacher and there is a good possibility of your becoming headmaster here. It is at walking distance and there is no expense for transportation. At Keezhillam, there is no one to fill the post vacated by Mr. C. T. Mathew. The salary they can give in one year may be equivalent to your one month's salary here. Still, this is a call from the church for a great need. My desire is that you resign your present job and go to Keezhillam to take up that job."

KOCHU KOCHU: "If that is Kunjichayan's desire, it is mine too."

Thus Kochu Kochu (P. C. Cheriyan) left for Keezhillam for an initial term of one year and ended up staying there for four decades. It was his hard work that elevated Keezhillam Middle School to one of the best high schools in Kerala. The growth of Mar Thoma High School, Keezhillam, was phenomenal, and the boarding school became famous for academic achievements, excellent discipline and competitive in sports and games.

Headmaster P. C. Cheriyan soon was elevated to the clergy status in Mar Thoma Church to fulfill the need of clergy in northern Travancore. The Lord blessed him with a perfect life partner, Kunjamma, who happened to have trained with Leyamma at Palghat Ashram.

Chackochy (P. C. Chacko), the older brother of the Rev. P. C. Cheriyan, had already moved to Keezhillam and was teaching in the grade school. While the two women who became the respective spouses of these brothers had come from different homes and circumstances, each had no difficulty in becoming a member of the extended family. Initially, both couples lived under the same roof and did not even consider having separate homes until P. C. George himself convinced them to do so.

P. C. Chacko was a soft-spoken man and a model teacher at the Keezhillam primary school until his early demise at the age of fifty. His beloved wife, Mariamma, also a schoolteacher, was pregnant with their fifth child at the time of his death. Mariamma continued with her responsibility of bringing up the children in Christian faith and discipline. Their older sons were named, P. C. Cheriyan and P. C. George. The third son was Thomas Jacob, and the girls were Annamma and Aleyamma. In the final years of Mariamma, the Rev. P. C. Cheriyan family moved back to fill the void created by all of the children moving out from Mariamma's home. Once again, they were under a single roof.

During his four decades of service in Keezhillam, the Rev. P. C. Cheriyan taught generations of students from all over Kerala and earned the love and respect from all who came to know him there. His students have gone to the four corners of the world. The honorable metropolitan of Mar Thoma Church, the Most Rev. Mar Chrysostom, said to my wife when he met us in an elevator in Florida: "Wherever I go in the world, I see Rev. P. C. Cheriyan's children." He might have exaggerated a little, but the Rev. P. C.

Cheriyan and Kunjamma had nine children, and those children and their own offspring indeed are spread out internationally. Here is a listing:

The oldest son, George Cheriyan, is settled with his wife, Jaya, in Trivandrum after retiring as the chief engineer at the Kerala State Electricity Board. Both are busy with altruistic activities of their own.

Molly, with her husband, Dr. Thomas Mathew, and two daughters, is in the mission field in Orissa. The hospital and a school that the couple established in this very poor region of the country continue to be a blessing to so many.

Susy, along with her husband, Raju, is in the mission field in the state of Tamil Nadu, continuing to serve in the school and engineering college.

Leyamma (my wife) retired as a pediatrician and enjoys her short-term international medical missions to Kenya, Zambia, and Mexico. She is actively involved in the multifaceted missions of the local church too.

Mammachen, a pediatrician along with Usha, is in Newfoundland, Canada, serving the health care needs of children.

Thampi and his wife, Geetha, live in the United States in Indianapolis, Indiana. They are very much involved in the activities of a local church.

Kunjumol, along with Pankle, after retiring from work in Bahrain, is settled in Trivandrum and is involved in teaching Sunday school and in other activities of the church.

Thomaskutty, after retiring from the Agriculture Department, has taken up full-time mission work in Andhra Pradesh. Preetha, his wife, is very much active in the music ministry of the local church.

Avarachan continues the legacy of his parents in Mundakapadam, where he lives with his wife, Annie. He is the connecting link for all the siblings to Mandiram and is their representative in every social function for the past few decades. He and his son both work in an established firm in Kerala as trusted CPAs.

It is worthy to note that all of them are active in their own way in serving the Lord. God has abundantly blessed the generations of the "orphans of Mundakapadam." I can echo the statement of the writer of the Psalms: "I have been young, and now am old; Yet I have not seen the righteous forsaken, Nor his descendants begging bread" (Psalm 37:25).

Mr. George Cheriyan, the eldest son of the Rev. P. C. Cheriyan, wrote the following in memory of his dad:

> For all nine children born to Rev. P. C. Cheriyan of Keezhillam, in case there is a reincarnation into this beautiful earth, to be born to the same parents, into the simple and peaceful surroundings with all its limited resources would be considered an immense blessing.
>
> Ours was an "open house" where the doors were open for anyone at any time to walk in. There were many friends from various categories who could walk in and participate in a meal without notice, friends who could even at night arrive and spend a night with us and parents of some students at boarding home, who would spend few days at a time sharing our limited resources were all well received and taken care of by mom and us the children. According to our dad, guests were to be treated like angels from God. Social, family or economic status of the guest did make no difference in the way one was treated at our home. We learned from our parents the basic lesson to share what we have, during our childhood.
>
> It was from our dad who taught us that individual is indebted to society. It's better to give than to receive and that by loving God and also His children, we can enjoy heaven here on

earth. Incidentally he was our teacher as well as our preacher" (from the Malayalam-language publication *Rev. P. C. Cherian Book of Memories*).

Not long after retirement, the Rev. P. C. Cheriyan became ill, and he passed away in March 1978. Mrs. P. C. Cheriyan soon moved to their original home in Manganam and stayed close to the sevinees in Mandiram. She continued to be a blessing to all her children and grandchildren as well as to those around her. She passed away at the ripe age of eighty-six in December 2001.

The Rev. and Mrs. P. C. Cheriyan, 1975

CHAPTER 14

Two Houses Separated by a Small Earthen Boundary and Two Families Bound in Christian Love

*T*he Puthuparambil house and the Peedikayil house were next to each other, separated by a small earthen boundary. The Christian love that bound the neighbors in these two households was tighter than anyone can describe. The Puthuparambil house was the abode for P.C. George, his two brothers, and their youngest sister, who had lost their parents at a very early age. Their maternal grandparents were there to take care of them for a few short years. Their neighbors at the Peedikayil house were two brothers and two younger sisters living with their parents.

It was the love from good neighbors that kept the boys and their sister at the Puthuparambil house going. Poverty only made the bond tighter, and the Christian love between these families blessed them both. The older brother in the Peedikayil house was P. A. Abraham, who became a physician and continued to serve at Christian Fellowship Hospital in Rajnandgaon, Chhattisgarh until his death. His younger brother, Abraham Varghese, also became a physician and served at Mandiram Hospital for about ten years after retiring from Christian Medical College, Vellore, in southern India. Both brothers wrote of their recollections in the Mandiram Platinum Jubilee souvenir that was published in September 2008.

Scanning through the memories of these two men, one can see the influence exerted upon their lives by their neighbors and friends, the four Puthuparambil siblings. Dr. P. A. Varghese recounted his love for the food at the Puthuparambil house in that article. Apparently he preferred to eat at the Puthuparambils than at the Peedikayils. As a young boy it was hard for him to see the poverty as a barrier at all. His mom outwitted him by sending food to the Puthuparambil home in advance without his knowledge and letting him eat it there, thinking that it was food from the Puthuparambils.

He recounted another incident where his leg was caught in a barbed wire fence he had attempted to jump over, making him hang there screaming in pain. All three of the Puthuparambil brothers ran to him to help; they extracted him from the barbed wire and carried him on their shoulders to the clinic a couple of miles away. All the while, the boy was giving them orders as who should carry him: "Now Muttan Ashan [George]; now Kochu Ashan [Chackochy]; and now Kochu-Kochu Ashan [P. C. Cheriyan]." Their love and affection knew no bounds. They reached the clinic, where his wounds were cleaned and taken care of.

His dad was very choosy about the company that the boy and his brother kept. Going out with George and his brothers was always okay. The close association with George exposed them to all sorts of spiritual and social reformation activities.

One day, when his grandparents were still alive, George listened to a lecture on the deleterious effects of alcohol on health and family life. That evening he climbed up a ladder that was fixed to a palm tree in their yard and cut down its flower stock, causing the income to the family to cease. His grandmother was in tears, but he consoled her, saying that God would provide.

George always had a large number of young followers who came from nearby villages such as Manganam, Puthuppally, Erikadu, Ancheri, and Thottakkadu. He conducted regular Bible study early on Sunday mornings. Those who were from far off would come on Saturday evening and stay at Mandiram to attend the Sunday classes. One morning as they gathered for the class, George announced, "Open your Bibles to Acts, chapter twenty-nine. We are going to study from there." They turned pages, but they saw that the book of Acts had only twenty-eight chapters. Then he announced that they, being followers of Jesus, should write the next chapter by their actions, doing what Jesus left unfinished.

George spoke continually about the dignity of labor. P. A. Varghese and another boy, M. A. John, Mooleparambil, were deputed to get out on the street and collect cow dung every day. For one full season these two boys started at Mandiram Junction and walked all the way to Puthuppally with the basket between them, collecting cow dung from the road. From Puthuppally they would walk to Manarcad Junction, and from there to Kanjikuzhy, and then back to Mandiram Junction. By this time they would have a full load of cow dung that they would proudly deposit in their compost pit at Mandiram.

George used to take his friends for a walk up Ashramam Hill and sit down at the top to pray with them. This was before Christava Ashramam was founded.

The two Peedikayil brothers soon became actively involved in going around the neighborhood collecting rice and money for Mandiram on a regular basis. During their summer vacation time, they would travel as far as Vakathanam to collect paddy from the rice farmers during the harvest season.

George's personal integrity was illustrated in an incident that Dr. Varghese wrote about. One day they were walking in the hot sun visiting homes. At Varghese's request, George had to open the folded umbrella that he was carrying under his arm. The umbrella was full of holes. George commented, "When I was employed as a teacher I had money to buy umbrella, but now as I am a full time volunteer for Mandiram, I am short of money." He did not want to spend even a small amount for personal use!

Dr. Abraham Varghese, the younger brother of Dr. P. A. Abraham, also recounted his memories in the Mandiram Platinum Jubilee souvenir. During the initial planning period of Mandiram, Dr. Varghese was too young to participate. Soon he, too, got involved in the *Pidiyari* and paddy collection for the support of Mandiram. He recounts his numerous trips through the neighborhood visiting many houses along with his companions, Mooleparambil Thommachen and Nagapurathu Cheriyachen. That experience helped him to get to know his own community at an early age. It helped the public to get directly involved in the support of Mandiram.

One year he went to Vakathanam, a nearby village, during the harvest season. This time P. C. George went along. They went in a country boat and stayed at the home of Kattil Kunjoonju and his wife, Baby. Kunjunju was full of humor, and Baby was the incarnation of true hospitality. All day they would continue visiting houses and collecting paddy. In the evening, after dinner, there would be singing, discussions, and sharing of experiences. For Dr. Abraham Varghese, these were memorable experiences from childhood.

At times they had some unpleasant experiences also. Dr. P. A. Abraham has mentioned one such experience in his autobiography (he refers to P. C. George as George Sir): "One day I was fed up with the shabby treatment from people and I told George Sir, 'why should we come all the way here to get these abuses?' With a smile George Sir replied, 'we are teaching them their duty toward the poor and the needy, even if they do not give anything to us now. My be more than teaching them, we are learning the discipline of love and sacrifice ourselves that could never be erased from our tender minds.'" Surely those memories of the youngsters were never erased from their minds.

P. C. George made a great impression on these youth through his Bible classes. In a multicultural society like India, his approach to other religions and cultures was unusual. He stressed the importance of respect for and dialogue with other religions. Through diagrams on a blackboard, he explained that God has been revealing Himself to mankind from early times. Different religions were the different ways in which people responded to God's revelations. This was a much needed message for the society where he lived.

George was frequently invited to various churches in the area to lead the worship service or to speak during the service. Dr. Abraham Varghese had the opportunity to accompany George on several of these speaking assignments. At times George would encourage the youngster to be the speaker too!

Dr. Varghese considered George a visionary who lived ahead of his time. In his short span of life, George accomplished a series of great things for his community. Apart from starting the Agathi Mandiram, he pioneered the cooperative society of Manganam and catalyzed the religious and social revival in the community. He was a counselor in several families, and because of his involvement, many families were saved from being broken up. Recognizing the harmful effects of alcohol on health and family, he started the antialcohol movement. He was a man of prayer with a great faith in God. The motto of Mandiram is "By Faith We Live." It is written on the entrance to the main building. Dr. Varghese considers George a great mentor for him and wrote this caption under George's photo in his album: "A Spiritual Volcano."

Students from George's Bible classes grew up to take on important challenges in life. Dr. Varghese mentioned a few names: Mr. M. A. John; Mr. V. C. Varghese; Dr. P. A. Abraham; Mr. C. I. Itty; Dr. Mathew P. John; Rev. Prof. K. C. Mathew; Mr. T. C. Oommen; and Mr. N. K. Chacko.

George wanted Dr. P. A. Varghese to serve in Mandiram Hospital. But Dr. Varghese saw a greater need for his service in the non-Christian area of northern India and continued to serve there until his recent demise.

Dr. Abraham Varghese, after retiring from his meritorious service at Christian Medical College, Vellore, decided to return to Manganam, where he served in Mandiram Hospital for ten years.

Reflections of a Family Member: What Is in a Name?

By Leyamma Cheriyan Mathew, MD; FAAP (wife of the author and daughter of the Rev. P. C. Cheriyan)

hile visiting my elder brother, George, in Trivandrum, I saw a handwritten letter addressed to him from my Valiappachen (uncle), Mr. P. C. George. (George was named after P. C. George.) It was written almost sixty-five years ago; this letter from uncle to nephew is well preserved and treasured by my brother.

The opening sentence of the letter is about me. He is talking about his little niece, named after his beloved sister Leyamma. He describes the way I tried to keep a distance from him while watching everything he did. His beloved sister's namesake showing her presence in the same house must have brought back lot of memories to Valiappachen's mind. As Valiappachen passed away while I was still a toddler, I do not have many memories about him. I remember standing at his side, softly touching his legs that were raised up on the handles of the recliner at the front porch of the old house. I have vivid memories of the perfumes and flowers and the huge crowd at his funeral. Seeing the handwritten letter from him talking about me, these many years later, brought goose bumps to me!

Sevinee Leyamma passed away at the age of thirty-one, several years before my birth. I am so honored and at the same time humbled to be named after this noble woman. It is not a simple task to live up to a name that had such a profound impact on so many during such a short life span. As I was growing up, I had the opportunity to meet many men and women whose lives were touched by Leyamma. Her name was a synonym for service. She was a friend of the poor, destitute, orphans, disabled, and marginalized. She was a great homemaker and manager with excellent leadership qualities.

Leyamma's untimely and early demise was the major inspiration for the inception of Mandiram Hospital. And once I was in medical school, everyone in my family decided that Dr. Leyamma would be at Mandiram Hospital. They could not think of seeing me working anywhere else. Sure enough, as soon as I finished medical school, I was appointed a junior medical officer at Mandiram Hospital. For a short period I stayed with the sevinees who were the coworkers of Leyamma at Mandiram. This was a time I personally witnessed the love, devotion, and hard work by these women who had dedicated their whole life for the service of the poor. Their life pattern was a true extension of Leyamma's example. And in a way, their life was an extension of Leyamma's life at Mandiram.

My stay with the sevinees at Mandiram gave me ample opportunity as an adult to see firsthand the operation of Agathi Mandiram. Interacting with the residents who came from various family, religious, caste, and economic backgrounds—but lived under the same roof—was a novel experience for them as well as me. What brought them together was a common link: an insatiable hunger for someone to love and care for them. There were men and women from well-to-do families, where they had found themselves out of place. Dementia and altered mental status often turned some elderly into outcasts from their own homes. Incurable illnesses and non-healing wounds were the reason for some to be on the streets and later in

Mandiram. Having a roof over their heads and a group of dedicated staff to lovingly take care of them around the clock was far more than they could ask for.

Relearning the basic social skills to get along with the rest of the residents was a tough job for some. Learning to trust the staff and other residents was a novel idea for many of these men and women. The sevinees' unwavering faith, selfless service, full dedication, and perseverance went a long way in developing trust among the residents.

Some of the residents were assigned to certain chores in the day-to-day activities of Mandiram. Those among the residents who were physically able and mentally stable were ready and willing to assist others as much as they could. Their chores were as simple as picking up the newspaper from the gate and bringing it to the office or as complicated as digging the graves to bury those who died at Mandiram.

Only by staying at Mandiram for several months was I able to get to know some of these residents at a closer range, including Palai Velliappan, Pillachan, and Aymanom Mariamma. They were all characters with interesting backgrounds and heartwarming stories.

Once I got married, we shifted our residence to the original Puthuparambil house next to the Mandiram campus. This had been home for P. C. George and P. C. Leyamma during their whole earthly lives. It was here that the idea for a home for the poor had first materialized. The first inmate was accommodated under a thatched extension to this home. This was where men and women of faith met and shed their tears in prayer for the sake of the poor and destitute in the community. This was where many prayer meetings and Bible studies were conducted. And this was where Leyamma learned the basic lessons in cooking out of necessity and entertained many a guest who came at odd times of the day to visit her brother George.

This old structure had housed several generations on my dad's side. It could have been a historic monument. This was the place where the dreams of two orphans were realized, where prayers of a few ordinary people on their knees were answered, where shelter, love, and care were given to sick and lonely by Leyamma and George, foreshadowing the Mandiram to be established shortly thereafter. But the tangible structure fell to the elements and disrepair; it was demolished a few years ago. The underlying property is awaiting God's leading for the next mission to be established there in His honor.

Leyamma was not a very common name. The only Leyamma a lot of people knew was P. C. Leyamma of Mundakapadam Mandiram. There were several occasions when people meeting me for the first time were reminded of P. C. Leyamma. I gratefully remember the short period when I worked as a junior doctor in Mandiram Hospital. The early passing of Leyamma because of the lack of timely medical care for a treatable infectious disease, cholera, had placed her loving brother George in deep sorrow—and it was from the depth of that sorrow that he resolved to plan for a hospital in Manganam. My cousin Aniyankunju (Dr. P. C. George) also worked in this hospital for a few years; he is the son of Mr. P. C. Chacko and is George's namesake.

Carrying the name of a person of the caliber of Sevinee Leyamma makes me humble. It often reminds me of the great heritage and her wonderful example in serving the sick, the needy, and the marginalized. As the niece of one who died serving those who did not have anyone else to go to, I carry her name often with some fear of falling short of expectations about me.

As a Christian, I carry the name of the one who paid the ultimate price with His life for those who least deserved it. The thought often makes me ponder: Am I truly representing my Master, whose name I carry?

What is in a name?

Part of the Rev. P. C. Cheriyan family, 1976

CHAPTER 16

Quotable Quotes from P. C. George

P. C. George was a man of great knowledge in many fields. The following quotations are from him. They testify to the depth of his faith as well as his knowledge.

"Any assignment, however boring it is, if it is for the building of the heavenly kingdom, can be done with new vigor."

"It seems that I am one with the secrets and working order of the whole universe."

"I have nothing but simple faith as my working capital."

"Unity among denominations should begin at the level of laity, not the clergy; they will follow soon."

"Showing mercy to the refugees from ships that were shattered in life's storms is never too much; their sorrows are immeasurable."

"Physicians can help to heal body aches; food and drink can quench hunger and thirst; words of consolation can heal heart aches; and friendship can heal the burdens of loneliness."

"It seems like I have witnessed more death than most of you!"

"A true home is not just a building for birth, death, dining, and sleeping; its pillars are contentment, cleanliness, love, and knowledge."

"He bore our hurts on Him; we, too, should do the same for others."

"The spiritual aspect of public service should be evident through creative projects."

"Please make a list of my shortcomings and give it to me."

"True enjoyment is when I take rest after a busy day of hard work."

"God and man became true to me through my work at Mandiram."

"Our hearts are enlightened when we meditate on God's love."

"He who has many friends is truly rich."

"Trust in God; trust in the goodness in others; trust in each other. Lack of this trust is the root cause of all failures."

"At times twenty-four hours in a day seems not enough for my prayers."

"We should not carry the burden of sin; it is God's job. He is ready to bear our burdens."

While going around raising a large fund for a project, someone asked George, "What is your secret in raising large funds?" To this he replied, "My secret of success is having no secrets."

CHAPTER 17

Looking Ahead

*E*verything about Mundakapadam Village has changed. The population has grown several fold in the past few decades. The standard of living has gone up. Educational institutions sprang up everywhere, and all in the community have access to better health care facilities. Public and private modes of transportation have grown quickly. Kottayam Puthuppally Road has become one of the busiest routes, with many private buses and several state transport buses traversing the route. Bullock carts are hard to find, even in the small villages.

The small house in which the Puthuparambil siblings lived is there no more. The author of this book and his wife—daughter of the Rev. P. C. Cheriyan and namesake of Leyamma—stayed in that house for a year in 1971–72. And Mrs. P. C. Cheriyan, along with her youngest son, Abraham Cheriyan, stayed there from 1979 till her death in 2001. That noble home, which should have been preserved as a historical monument, went into disrepair and was demolished. The original Mandiram, which was started as an attachment to the side of that house, had moved to its permanent place next door in a new building. A dispensary that originally was in a thatched building near Mandiram also was moved to another part of the expanding property, and there it was established as the Mandiram

Hospital. It caters to the medical needs of thousands of men and women in the region.

More and more projects were envisioned, and new buildings have mushroomed out all over Mandiram Hill. Now there is comfortable accommodation for over one hundred residents in Mandiram. The chapel stands out near the main entrance to the compound, providing worship and prayer services every day. An administrative building and the housing for the sevinees are nearby. Balikabhavan provides supervised shelter for several young girls. The Rev. P. C. Cheriyan Memorial Library is used well by various residents of the home. Juhanon Memorial Home for the senior citizens is nearby, along with several other assisted retirement home units. Leyamma Memorial School of Nursing has been providing nursing training for many years now.

Mandiram Hospital has grown into a multi-specialty hospital with several dedicated men and women following the Master Physician in their vocation of providing healing to the body and spirit. A mental health center stands out at the top of Mandiram Hill.

All in all, what tremendous growth has resulted from the small beginning. What an example of God putting a dream in His children's hearts and fulfilling it!

Modes of communication saw the fastest growth during the past decade in this area. It is not uncommon to see a person carrying more than one cell phone or else a single cell phone with multiple SIM cards in use! Cable TV and the Internet have brought the world closer than ever. Huts and dilapidated shelters were replaced by huge houses and multilevel flats that could house hundreds of families. Small churches were replaced by huge structures, proudly showing off the earthly riches of the churches. Toddy shops along the roadside that used to sell alcohol that was fermented from palm tree juice were replaced by foreign liquor stores run by the state government. With the tremendous material prosperity that the state experienced, one could not miss noticing the loss in moral and spiritual values, with increasing corruption in high places, including in the church. There was a drop in family prayers and a rapid increase in the divorce rate and suicide rate in "God's own country." With the advent of modern communication modes, it was easy for the conservative, traditional Eastern youth to rapidly follow all that is the worst in the Western culture while carefully avoiding all its good aspects!

A huge number of Malayalees have migrated to foreign countries during the past four decades in search of better educational and job opportunities. This out-migration of the masses benefited the homeland with an enormous economic uplift from money sent back to the region. These men and women with a resolve to work hard and save were eager to invest their hard-earned money in their homeland of Kerala to build big houses, foster businesses, and provide for their dear ones who remained there. Many who had to leave their spouses and children in Kerala while working in a foreign land sacrificed a lot for their well-being. Little did many of them realize that while they were providing their children with affluence, they adversely affected the children in their formative years by not being present to give direct supervision. It was a real eye-opening experience for the diaspora to return to the homeland of their desires and dreams and discover that the whole culture had changed! To their utter surprise, now they are foreigners in their own land.

One could recall the experience of walking along the village road at sunset listening to the chants and prayers that came from neighboring homes. With the kerosene lamp lit and placed at the front room of the house, people would sit around and offer their evening prayers. From the homes of Hindus one could expect chanting like this:

Rama Rama Rama Rama Rama Pahimam
Ram padam cherane Mukunda Rma Pahimam

Or from a Christian home:

Parane nin thiru munpil varunnoree samaye
Sariyay prardhana cheyvan thunaye thannarulka.

Things have changed now. Every home has electricity and twenty-four-hour television. Religious chanting has been replaced with the loud music from these electronic tubes, and prayer has taken a back burner!

Problems and issues in Mundakapadam or any other township in Kerala are different from those at the time when P. C. George and Leyamma were alive. Issues in an affluent, educated, secular, and morally bankrupt society are many and are harder to deal with.

Alcoholism, with its extreme harmful effects, has eroded the society here. It is unfortunate that the church is not taking a stronger stand against this social evil.

Premarital counseling and education in family values are of paramount importance in dealing with the ever-increasing divorce rate.

The Christian family unit provides an important influence. Martin Luther called it the home church. This is where one learns the basic and fundamental lessons in Christian faith and Christian living.

Longevity has gone up and the aging population is growing by leaps and bounds, thanks to better health care and nutrition. Unfortunately, this is the segment of society that needs increased support too. More and more elderly are left to care for themselves. Loneliness at any age is bad, but at old age it is miserable. Properly supervised and managed retirement homes and assisted-living facilities are needed. The church must take a leading role in this.

Catering to the needs of the youth is another key area, one which the church should address. Whether in the structure and form of the worship, the day and time of worship, or the use of instrumental music in worship, it is high time that the church recognizes the aspirations and taste of the youth. The church must change with the times to accommodate the youth: they are the future church leaders.

Love your neighbor—that is the great commandment Jesus gave us, and that is exactly what George and Leyamma followed. They loved the least, the lost, and the marginalized in the society. They shared from their limited resources to make the lives of the poorest somewhat bearable. George and Leyamma were far ahead of their time, and they were not afraid to make changes wherever changes were necessary. They extended their love outside their close circles, beyond the religious, cultural, caste, or age dimensions. On account of their experience of growing up as orphans of Mundakapadam, they placed themselves in the powerful hands of the Almighty, to be used as instruments to serve hundreds of orphans that came through the portals of Mandiram in the following years.

George and Leyamma are waiting for their rewards when the Master tells them, "Well done my good and faithful servant. Whatever you have done for these little ones, you have done for me."

May you and I live by this commandment!

Appendix I

Historical Letters

Copies of these handwritten letters from P. C. George to his nephew, George Cheriyan, are published here for the first time. The author expresses his sincere thanks to Georgekuttychayan!

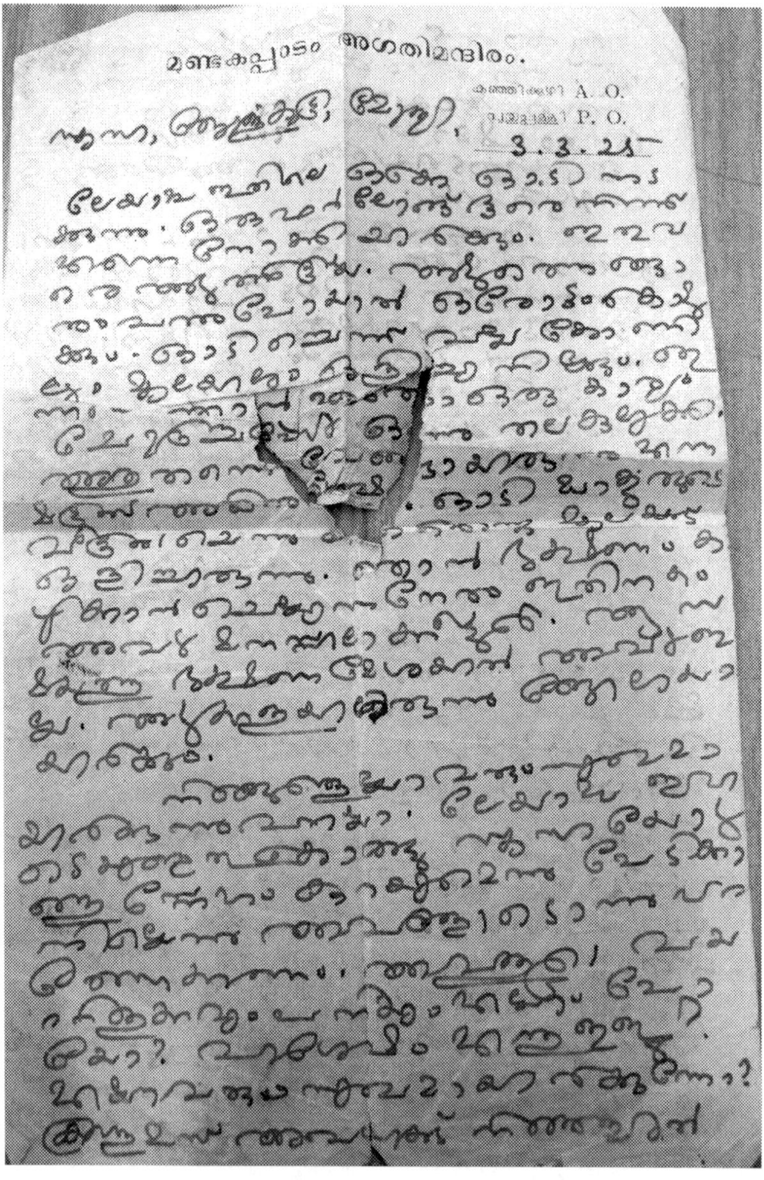

മുണ്ടകപ്പാടം അഗതിമന്ദിരം.

A. O.
P. O.

3.3.25

എന്ന, അച്ഛമ്മ, ...,

George Cheriyan still gets emotional and teary eyed when reading the letters from his Valiyappachan, Mr. P.C. George.

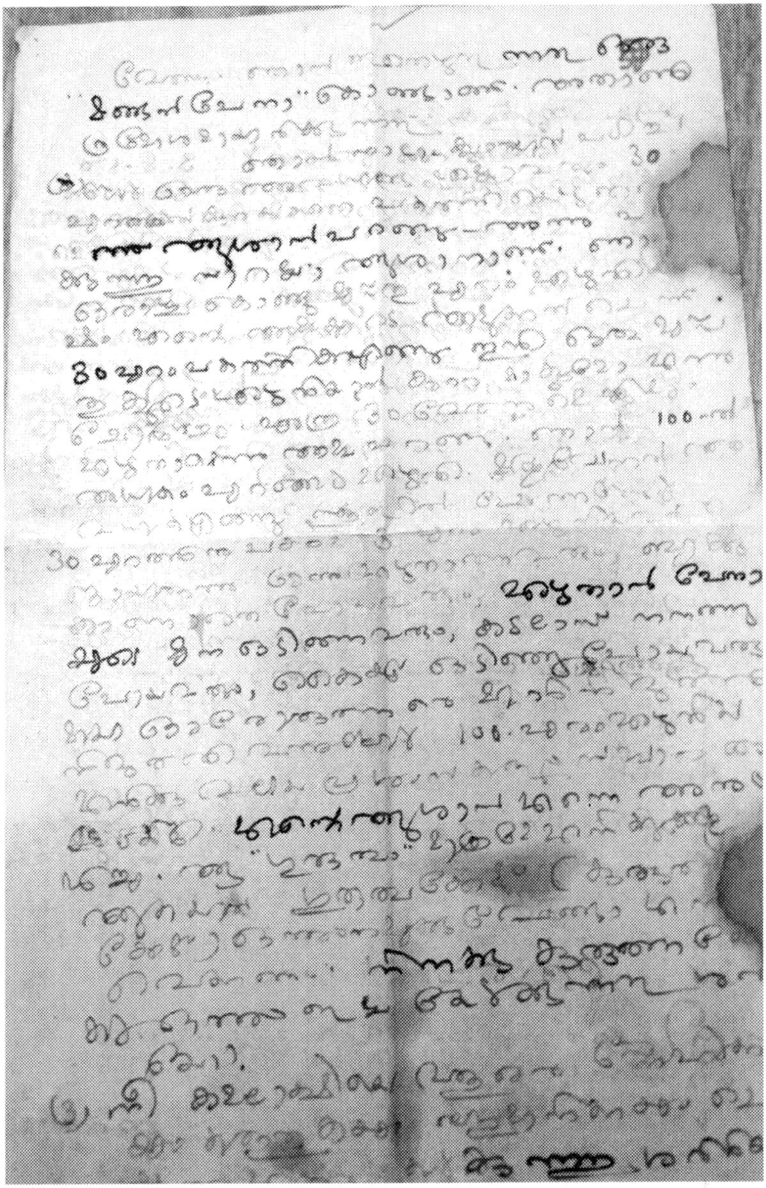

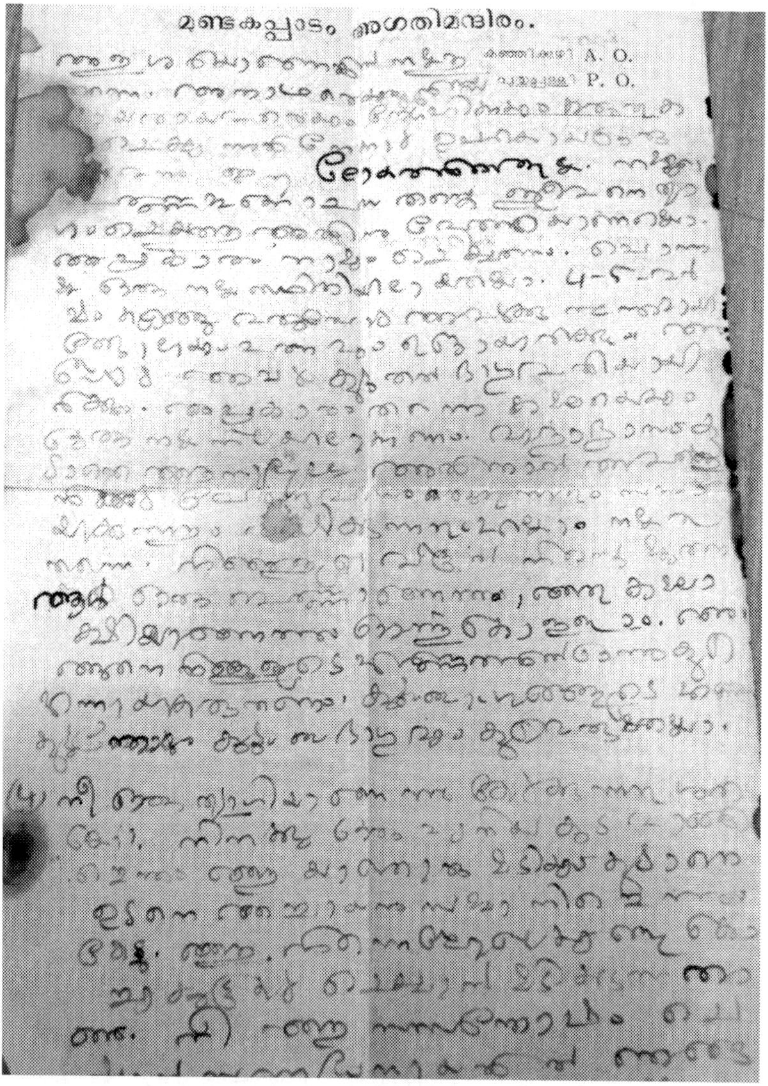

മുണ്ടകപ്പാടം അഗതിമന്ദിരം.
A. O.
P. O.